HUNTER DAVIES

Twelve fairly interesting things about Hunter Davies:

1 Very fond of stamps
2 Author of fifteen books
3 Quite fond of railways
4 Comes from Carlisle
5 Has been editor of *The Sunday Times magazine*
6 Is married to Margaret Forster and has three children
7 Has written a biography of the Beatles
8 Is terribly fond of lists
9 Has written a biography of William Wordsworth
10 Is a trained teacher
11 Wrote the film *Here We Go, Round the Mulberry Bush*
12 Has a sore knee just now but hopes to play football
   again very soon

BOOK
OF
BRITISH
LISTS

HUNTER DAVIES

Hamlyn Paperbacks

BOOK OF BRITISH LISTS
ISBN 0 600 20267 4

First published in Great Britain 1980
by Hamlyn Paperbacks
Copyright © 1980 by Hunter Davies

Hamlyn Paperbacks are published by
The Hamlyn Publishing Group Ltd,
Astronaut House,
Feltham,
Middlesex, England
(Paperback Division: Hamlyn Paperbacks,
Banda House, Cambridge Grove,
Hammersmith, London W6 OLE)

Typeset, printed and bound in Great Britain by
Hazell Watson & Viney Ltd, Aylesbury, Bucks

CONTENTS

viii

ACKNOWLEDGEMENTS

I should like to thank the following researchers for all the
help they have provided in the preparation of this book.
Jan Kaluza
Tamara Holboll
Nicholas Mason
Peter Wilby
Sheridan Morley
Caitlin Davies (age 16)
Jake Davies (age 14)
And all the authors and editors of the books and publications
mentioned.

INTRODUCTION

I suppose the most common list is a shopping list. That's a list all of us have compiled at some time, and some of us keep on compiling them, week after week. So imagine our surprise and delight when in the course of preparing this little book a lady wrote to us from Exeter and said that she collected shopping lists, picking them up from the floor of supermarkets and such like places and sticking them in her album. You'll find the first shopping list she found under 'L' for lists. Doubtless she has a list of the lists she's found, but we'll spare you that one.

Most of the day-to-day humdrum lists we make are pretty scruffy, written on the backs of envelopes, meaningful only to ourselves, and sometimes not even then as we stand and stare at the check-out counter, lost in our codes, confused by our abbreviations.

At the other extreme, you get Government lists. They endlessly pour out of every department, all of them terribly neat and beautifully tabulated with asterisks sprouting everywhere, teeming with information. The Department of Health and Social Security, like all major Ministries, publishes *Sectional Lists* – a hefty booklet which lists every list they publish. You can even get a list of all the Ministries which publish lists of lists. Are you still there?

I hope we haven't taken too many liberties in this book of lists, simplifying too much, trying to make our lists easy to read. A lot of our lists have been abstracted from Government and other official publications. Their terms of reference and definitions are not always what they seem to the layman, and you don't always know what they haven't counted, but there's gold in most of them, if you're prepared to pan long enough. Unless otherwise stated, the lists are correct up to January 1980.

One list I struggled hard to abstract was the top ten most frequent operations in hospitals, which seemed an easy enough question, until I found the answers were buried deep in a 426-page Department of Health report which listed, under a different name and number, 999 surgical operations. I compiled two lists in the end, which I hope make some sort of sense. See 'O' for Operations.

A lot of the lists are taken from published sources, such as the Government's *Social Trends*, but a lot are original, in the sense that they are based on our own researches, perhaps by the simple expedient of ringing up, say, Marks & Spencer and asking them for their best-selling single items, or asking ICI for its best-selling Dulux paint colour. You know such firms have such figures, hidden away somewhere, if only you can find the right person at the right time in the right frame of mind to dig them out. The book trade and the pop music industry give out their best-selling charts every week, but there are many more industries with equally interesting sales or popularity lists which never get published.

I've always been interested in lists. In every non-fiction book I've ever done I've always had lists at the end, tarting them up as appendices, unwilling to leave in my files all the off-beat information I've picked up on my researches and been unable to work in.

At the end of the Beatles biography, for example, I listed the Beatle songs most recorded by other people ('Yesterday' was top); in *The Glory Game*, which was about Tottenham Hotspur, I listed the first team's favourite newspapers (*The Sun* won); and in *A Walk Around the Lakes* I listed the most visited houses in the Lake District (Beatrix Potter's was first, just ahead of Wordsworth's). Over the years, I've had an enormous number of letters about these lists, even from people doing real academic research. Three people have used *The Glory Game* in Ph.D.s, using my daft questions to footballers as a comparison with professionals in other sports. I knew you'd be impressed.

But my wife wasn't impressed. She thinks lists are boring and can't understand anyone wanting to compile a *book* of lists, far less read one. It's a book for people who don't read books, so she says. I immediately started working this idea into a list. Muzak is for people who don't like music. Sliced bread is for people who don't like bread. Now, what other examples can I put in this list . . .?

I could defend lists by saying all knowledge is lists, which I think is a quote from Scott Fitzgerald. If not, I made it up.

Single facts don't get you very far. It's only when they are arranged in some sort of a pattern or order that they have any meaning. And that's when you start making lists. But I can't make too much of a case for the little lists in this book. They're meant to be fun, a Christmas stocking filler, lavatory reading if nothing else. (My wife also hates people who read on the lavatory.)

I started trying to organize this offering three years ago when I was editor of *The Sunday Times magazine*, but I couldn't find anyone to do the research. I wanted to run a weekly list, on any old subject which took our fancy. By 1980, having left the editorial chain, I started to do the research myself, and then got others to help. Michael Bateman, editor of 'Lifespan', kindly agreed to run one every week in his pages, which is how you might have seen one or two of these lists already in *The Sunday Times*.

By this time, the Americans, curses, had already brought out their *Book of Lists*, which did amazingly well in the States and also sold well here. Ours has the unique advantage of being totally British. Hurrah.

There are three sorts of lists in this book. Firstly, there are lists in some kind of factual order, such as the ten biggest counties in acreage. Then there are lists which are a grouping together under the same heading, such as Prime Ministers Who Were Adulterers. And finally there are lists of people's opinion. When we asked a famous person for his or her list of favourites, the answers all had to be British, and quite right too. Some may well be rubbish, but then it's all good British rubbish...

London
March 1980

ADULTERERS

We could have chosen any profession, as no calling has a monopoly, but we decided to look at prime ministers, especially those long dead.

Prime ministers
who were adulterers

Gladstone is said to have maintained that he knew eleven Prime Ministers in his lifetime, seven of whom were adulterers. It's a list which is hard to assemble, at least with complete certainty, as several of the allegations have still never been properly documented. (There are rumours about Gladstone himself, and the prostitutes he 'befriended'.) The following list has been checked with A. J. P. Taylor who says that in each case there is either reasonable proof, such as a court case (certain), or contemporary reports which strongly suggest at least one adulterous affair (probable).

Duke of Devonshire – (certain)
Lord John Russell – (certain)
Duke of Wellington – (certain)
George Canning – (probable)
Lord Grey – (certain)
Lord Melbourne – (probable)
Lord Aberdeen – (probable)
Lord Palmerston – (certain)
Benjamin Disraeli – (certain)
David Lloyd George – (certain)
Herbert Asquith, Earl of Oxford – (probable)

ADVERTISING

MEAL (Marketing Week)

D'Arcy MacManus and Masius was the biggest advertising agency in Britain in 1979, in terms of money spent, displacing J. Walter Thompson which dropped to fourth position. Saatchi and Saatchi, now the country's best-known agency as far as the general public is concerned, thanks to its work for the Tory Party, had a drop in expenditure, partly due to the ITV strike, but it still came third.

Top ten advertising agencies for 1979

'79	'78	agency	£m 1978	1979	% change
1	(2)	D'Arcy MacManus & Masius	44·7	50·7	+13·5
2	(4)	McCann Erickson	42·9	45·2	+5·6
3	(3)	Saatchi & Saatchi Garland Compton	47·1	43·6	−7·4
4	(1)	J. Walter Thompson	45·4	43·4	−4·4
5	(6)	Collett Dickenson Pearce	30·2	34·1	+12·8
6	(5)	Ogilvy Benson & Mather	31·7	31·5	−0·6
7	(8)	Young & Rubicam	18·6	21·4	+15·4
8	(7)	Ted Bates	21·2	21·3	+0·5
9	( )	Allen Brady Marsh	14·2	19·9	+39·9
10	(10)	Wasey Campbell Ewald	17·4	18·2	+4·8

AGRICULTURE

Agricultural land in the UK
1976 – in thousand hectares

Total agricultural area	18 988
Arable land	6 975

Rough grazing (including common rough grazing)	6 513
Permanent grassland	5 081
Total woodland on agricultural holdings	239
All other land on agricultural holdings	180

Use of arable land

Total	6 975
Barley	2 182
Grassland	2 139
Wheat	1 231
Fodder crops	285
Oats	235
Potatoes	222
Sugar beet	206
Vegetables	206
Fruit	68
Bare fallow	65
Other	59
Other cereals	37
Flowers and nursery stock	16
Lucerne	14
Hops	6
Mustard	4

ALCOHOL CONSUMPTION

Quantities of spirits
per person, per year
Book of Numbers, Heron House, 1979

Canada	12·6 (pints)
W. Germany ⎱ Netherlands ⎰	11·9

Sweden	10·3
USA	
France	9·1
Spain	
Ireland	7·2
Italy	7·0
Switzerland	
Norway	6·5
Denmark	6·3
Austria	5·8
Belgium	5·2
Australia	4·5
UK	3·5

Quantities of beer
per person, per year
Brewers' Society

W. Germany	259·4 (pints)
Australia	250·1
Belgium	237·1
Ireland	230·6
Denmark	227·0
UK	207·0
Austria	182·7
Canada	151·2
USA	151·0
Netherlands	138·9
Switzerland	127·8
Sweden	103·5
Spain	79·9
France	79·7
Norway	79·4
Japan	62·3
Italy	22·5

When it comes to beer, we're middle of the road, not swerving too badly.

Quantities of wine
per person, 1965

Book of Numbers, Heron House

Italy	189·2
France	182·5
Spain	133·8
Switzerland	77·3
Austria	61·8
W. Germany	51·0
Belgium	30·3
Australia	19·7
Netherlands	18·0
Sweden	13·5
UK	9·2

ATHLETICS

Olympic Gold Medals won by British athletes since the
modern games began in 1896.

1896	none
1900	Alfred Tysoe (800 metres)
	Charles Bennett (1 500 metres)
1904	none
1908	Wyndham Halswell (400 metres)
	Timothy Ahearne (triple jump)
1912	Arnold Jackson (1 500 metres)
	4 × 100 metres relay team (David Jacobs, Harold Macintosh, Victor d'Arcy and William Applegarth)
1920	Albert Hill (800 metres)
	Albert Hill (1 500 metres)
	Percy Hodge (3 000 metres steeplechase)
	4 × 400 metres relay team (Cecil Griffiths, Robert Lindsay, John Ainsworth-David, Guy Butler)

1924	Harold Abrahams (100 metres)
	Eric Liddell (400 metres)
	Douglas Lowe (800 metres)
1928	Douglas Lowe (800 metres)
	Lord Burghley (400 metres hurdles)
1932	Thomas Hampson (800 metres)
	Thomas Green (50 000 metres walk)
1936	4 × 400 metres relay team (Frederick Wolff, Godfrey Rampling, William Roberts, Godfrey Brown)
	Harold Whitlock (50 000 metres walk)
1948	none
1952	none
1956	Christopher Brasher (3 000 metres steeplechase)
1964	Ken Matthews (20 000 metres walk)
	Lynn Davies (long jump)
	Ann Packer (women's 800 metres)
	Mary Rand (women's long jump)
1968	David Hemery (400 metres hurdles)
1972	Mary Peters (women's pentathlon)
1976	none

BASTARDS

Purely in the old-fashioned, legal sense of course – people born, or assumed to have been born, out of wedlock. This list also includes orphans – people brought up in orphanages, the marital status of their parents being unclear.

William the Conqueror, 1027–1087, monarch
Sir Robert Walpole, 1676–1745, prime minister
T. E. Lawrence, 1888–1935, Arabist and author
Lord Melbourne, 1779–1848, prime minister
Ramsey MacDonald, 1866–1937, prime minister
Sir Henry Stanley, 1841–1904, journalist and explorer
Leslie Thomas, b. 1931 –   , author

BEAUTY

Miss United Kingdom

This competition has been held annually in Blackpool since 1958, and the first prize now totals £7 500, with the winner gaining automatic entry into the Miss World contest. Does it prove that the North has more beautiful ladies than the South?

1958	Eileen Sheridan, Walton-on-Thames
1959	Anne Thelwell, Heswall
1960	Hilda Fairclough, Lancaster
1961	Rosemarie Frankland, Lancaster
1962	Jackie White, Alvaston
1963	Diana Westbury, Ilkeston
1964	Ann Sidney, Parkstone
1965	Lesley Langley, London
1966	Jennifer Lowe, Warrington
1967	Jennifer Lewis, Leicester
1968	Kathleen Winstanley, Wigan
1969	Sheena Drummond, Tullibody
1970	Yvonne Ormes, Nantwich
1971	Marilyn Ward, New Milton
1972	Jenny McAdam, London
1973	Veronica Cross, London
1974	Helen Morgan, Barry
1975	Vicki Harris, London
1976	Carol Grand, Glasgow
1977	Madeleine Stringer, North Shields
1978	Ann Jones, Welshpool
1979	Carolyn Seaward, Plymouth

Miss World

Founded in 1951 by Eric D. Morley, the contest is held annually in London. It is watched by an adoring British public on TV so naturally has to be included in British lists as a British spectator sport.

1951	Kiki Haakonson (Sweden)
1952	May Louise Flodin (Sweden)
1953	Denise Perrier (France)
1954	Antigone Costanda (Egypt)
1955	Carmen Susana Duijm (Venezuela)
1956	Petra Schurmann (West Germany)
1957	Marita Lindahl (Finland)
1958	Penny Coelen (South Africa)
1959	Corine Rottschafer (Holland)
1960	Norma Cappegli (Argentina)
1961	Rosemarie Frankland (UK)
1962	Rina Lodders (Holland)
1963	Carole Crawford (Jamaica)
1964	Ann Sidney (UK)
1965	Lesley Langley (UK)
1966	Reita Faria (India)
1967	Madeleine Hartog-Bel (Peru)
1968	Penny Plummer (Australia)
1969	Eva Rueber-Staier (Austria)
1970	Jennifer Hosten ((Grenada)
1971	Lucia Petterle (Brazil)
1972	Belinda Green (Australia)
1973	Marji Wallace (USA)
1974	Helen Morgan (UK – resigned)
	Anneline Kriel (South Africa)
1975	Wilnelia Merced (Puerto Rico)
1976	Cindy Breakspeare (Jamaica)
1977	Mary Stavin (Sweden)
1978	Silvana Suarez (Argentina)
1979	Gina Swainson (Bermuda)

BLUE PLAQUES
GLC figures

There are 427 blue plaques on London houses, commemorating the fact that some famous person once lived there. Some lucky people are remembered by more than one plaque, having lived in different houses.

Three plaques

W. E. Gladstone	statesman
D. G. Rossetti	poet and painter
Lord Palmerston	statesman
W. M. Thackeray	novelist

Two plaques

Sir J. M. Barrie	novelist and dramatist
Elizabeth Barrett Browning	poet
Sir Isambard Kingdom Brunel	civil engineer
Joseph Chamberlain	statesman
Samuel Taylor Coleridge	poet
Benjamin Disraeli	statesman
George du Maurier	artist and writer
George Eliot	novelist
Henry Fielding	novelist
John Galsworthy	novelist
David Garrick	actor
John Richard Green	historian
Thomas Hardy	novelist
Thomas Hood	poet
William Morris	poet and artist
Lord Nelson	admiral
Samuel Pepys	diarist
George Bernard Shaw	dramatist
Richard Brinsley Sheridan	dramatist
Sir Hans Sloane	physician
Algernon Swinburne	poet
Sir Robert Walpole	statesman
William Wilberforce	philanthropist

Total number of plaques in each London borough

Westminster	195
Kensington and Chelsea	78
Camden	62
Tower Hamlets	18
Wandsworth	15
Hammersmith	9
Lambeth	9
Islington	8
Greenwich	6
Lewisham	5
Barnet	3
Bexley	3
Croydon	3
Hackney	3
Richmond	3
Haringey	2
Southwark	2
Bromley	1
Hounslow	1
Redbridge	1

BOOKS

British book titles, 1979

There was a record number of books published in 1979: 41 940 different titles. According to the totals published by *The Bookseller*, which classifies them under subjects, fiction produced more titles than any other subject. These are the top twenty subjects:

Fiction	4 551
Political science and economy	3 364
Children's books	2 510
Medical science	2 510
School textbooks	2 144
Religion	1 509
History	1 421
Law and public administration	1 404
Engineering	1 334
Biography	1 236
Art	1 226
Literature	1 161
Natural sciences	1 157
Commerce	1 073
Education	1 024
Sociology	964
Poetry	788
Bibliography and library economy	723
Chemistry and physics	684
Travel and guide books	674

The total of 41 940 titles includes 9 086 reprints or new editions – but they form a smaller proportion than in previous years. They made up 30% of the titles in 1970 but have now dropped to 22%. As for the different subjects, only Art, Chemistry and physics, and Sociology books showed a decrease on the previous year. Children's books increased most, by 6·8%; while Fiction, which had fallen the year before, increased by 4%.

Best-sellers, 1979 – those most mentioned in *The Sunday Times* best-seller lists

The best-selling book of 1979 was *Life on Earth* by David Attenborough (BBC/Collins) which headed *The Sunday Times* non-fiction list 25 times.

The Country Diary of an Edwardian Lady by Edith Holden
(Webb & Bower/Michael Joseph) headed the list seven times,
after dominating it throughout 1978.

Clementine, the biography of Winston Churchill's wife by her
daughter, Mary Soames (Cassell), was second for eight weeks.

Mountbatten – Eighty Years in Pictures (Macmillan) was top of
the list for a fortnight, being published shortly after Lord
Mountbatten's murder.

Fiction

The Devil's Alternative by Frederick Forsyth (Hutchinson)
became No 1 novel on publication and headed the fiction list
for three months.

The Last Enchantment by Mary Stewart (Hodder) topped the
list for eight weeks.

The Master Mariner by Nicholas Monsarrat (Cassell) headed
the list for five weeks.

Good as Gold by Joseph Heller (Cape) was top for four weeks.

Proteus by Morris West (Collins) was top for three weeks.

The Sea, the Sea by Iris Murdoch (Chatto) was top for two
weeks.

Top ten all-time BBC publications

1	*America*	2 234 178
2	*The Ascent of Man*	1 618 698
3	*Civilization*	1 475 000
4	*Life on Earth*	1 040 599
5	*Blue Peter – 11th Book*	541 537
6	*Hold Down A Chord Book 1*	448 615
7	*Adventurous Cooking*	401 537
8	*Ten Classic Dishes*	370 236
9	*Jimmy Young Cook Book*	355 310
10	*Home Cooking*	333 356

It's easily forgotten how successful the BBC is in producing
books – far better than many a publisher, who do not have the

advantage of having successful TV programmes to publicize their titles. The above figures include paperback and hardback sales, both in the UK and abroad.

The ten oddest book titles

At the Frankfurt Book Fair, the world's biggest annual book fair with over 300 000 titles on display, a competition is held to find the world's oddest book title. In 1979 the Diagram Group of London awarded a bottle of champagne to David Martin of Basil Blackwell, who spotted the title which was judged number one.

1 *The Madam as Entrepreneur: Career Management in House Prostitution* (USA)
2 *How to Thoroughly Criticize the Gang of Four and Bring About a New Upsurge in the Movement to Build Tachai-Type Counties throughout the Country* (China)
3 *Gut Reaction – How to Live with your Intestinal Tract* (USA)
4 *100 Years of British Rail Catering* (UK)
5 *Buddhism in Fifteen Minutes* (Japan)
6 *Tasty Dishes from Waste Items* (USA)
7 *The Interpretation of Geological Time from the Evidence of Fossilized Elephant Droppings in Eastern Europe* (Poland)
8 *Having Fun with Rats* (USA)
9 *Ethics for Bureaucrats* (UK)
10 *Cooking with God* (USA)

The 1978 winner was a Japanese publication: *Proceedings of the Second International Workshop on Nude Mice*.

Bruce Robertson of the Diagram Group has been collecting his own private list at Frankfurt for ten years, but three years ago he asked all the publishers and book people visiting Frankfurt to send him the daftest titles they had seen. 'You get daft titles because you get daft publishers – but I bet all the titles on this year's list will sell for a long time. They're all

13

real, published books. The elephant droppings one is in four languages. Publishers are always very hopeful, I met an English publisher this year with a book he'd sold successfully in the USA, *Your Irish Ancestors*. He was trying to sell it to the Japanese, but not doing very well. . . .'

Children's best-sellers, 1979

This list, from *The Bookseller*, was compiled by the National Book League from answers from general and specialist members of the Children's Booksellers' Group of the Booksellers' Association in England and Wales. It is made up from paperback and hardback titles published in the year and sold in bookshops.

1 *Masquerade* by Kit Williams (Cape)
2 *I Like This Poem* ed. Kaye Webb (Puffin)
3 *The Haunted House* by Jan Pienkowski (Heinemann)
4 *Fungus The Bogeyman* by Raymond Briggs (Hamish Hamilton)
5 *Revolving Pictures* by Ernest Nister (Collins)
6 *Worzel Gummidge* by B. E. Todd (Puffin)
7 *A Day in the Life of Petronella Pig* by Tatiana Hauptmann (Benn)
8 *Simple Electronics* by Rev. G. C. Dobbs (Ladybird)
9 *The Whizzkid's Handbook* by Peter Eldin (Fontana)
10 *Sixteenth Book Blue Peter* by Biddy Baxter, Edward Barnes and John Adcock (BBC)

CABBIES

London taxi-cab drivers, according to their magazine *Cab Driver*, put Post Office van drivers at the top of their hate list in a 1980 survey. 'The biggest menace to other motorists,' so they say. They weren't very polite either about their second most hated species of driver on the roads, security van drivers – 'As thick as the armour plating they drive in.'

Cabbies' hate list

1 GPO van drivers
2 Security vehicle drivers
3 Swiss and Italian motorists
4 Juggernaut drivers
5 Newspaper van drivers
6 Cyclists
7 Men with pipes and dirty cars
8 Two, or more women in minis
9 Selfish taxi drivers
10 Nuns and rabbis (not necessarily together)

In reply, the Post Office said they'd never done such a survey, but if they did, cabbies would definitely be tops. 'The arrogance of taxi-drivers would put them in number one place on a list of lousy motorists.' So there.

CAMBRIDGE COLLEGES IN ORDER OF FOUNDATION

Another two-in-one list. Now you know the names of the Cambridge Colleges.

Peterhouse	1284	King's	1441
Clare	1326	Queen's	1448
Pembroke	1347	St Catharine's	1473
Gonville and Caius	1348	Jesus	1496
Trinity Hall	1350	Christ's	1505
Corpus Christi	1352	St John's	1511

Magdalene	1542	St Edmund's House	1896
Trinity	1546	Newhall	1954
Emmanuel	1584	Churchill	1960
Sidney Sussex	1596	Darwin	1964
Downing	1800	Wolfson	1965
Girton	1869	Fitzwilliam	1966
Newnham	1871	Clare Hall	1966
Selwyn	1882		

CARDS

The ten rarest packs of playing cards to be sold in Britain

1	Mantegna Tarot *c.* 1450	£15 000
2	Reign of James II *c.* 1690	£3 500
3	Love Mottoes *c.* 1710	£2 500
4	South Sea Bubble *c.* 1720	£2 500
5	Lives of the Saints *c.* 1700	£2 000
6	De Brianville Heraldic pack *c.* 1667/69	£2 000
7	Marlborough's Victories 1707	£1 700
8	Popish Plot 1679	£1 500
9	Lenthall Fortune Telling cards *c.* 1720	£1 500
10	Redmayne Geographical cards *c.* 1676 (41 cards out of a pack of 52)	£1 300

Playing cards are largely taken for granted. People do not realize that packs can range from as little as 21 cards to as many as 360 and that as well as Britain's traditional suit signs of hearts, diamonds, spades and clubs there are the additional continental suit motifs of leaves, acorns, bells, swords, cups, coins and batons. Apart from the traditionally designed packs used for ordinary card games, through the

16

ages packs have been produced with educational, political, religious, historical, geographical, heraldic, purely fanciful and amusing subject matters.

Collecting playing cards is now an established and growing hobby, with prices ranging from well under £5 for more modern packs to several thousands for older examples. Collectors' clubs have been formed and Stanley Gibbons, the London stamp people, have a department devoted to old and modern packs, and hold regular auctions.

CARS

In Britain

These figures of motor vehicles in the UK are based on the number of vehicle licences issued each year, from Department of Transport figures.

type of vehicle	thousands
Private cars & private vans	14 417
Motorcycles, scooters & mopeds	1 211
Goods	1 743
Agricultural tractors	408
Other vehicles	311
Public transport vehicles	111
All vehicles	18 201

Round the world

The USA has the highest number of cars per 1 000 of the population, but Japan has the highest increase – from one per 1 000 in 1953 to 180 per 1 000 in 1977. In 1977, six out of ten families in Great Britain had regular use of a car, and more than one family in ten had two or more cars. In Scotland, however, fifty-four per cent of families did not have a car, and only seven per cent had two or more cars.

Car ownership:
international comparison

| | number of cars per 1 000 population | | | | | |
	1953	1961	1966	1971	1976	1977
USA	288	345	400	427	510	530
Sweden	60	175	241	291	351	346
W. Germany	22	95	179	247	308	326
France	47	135	210	261	300	315
Italy	13	50	125	209	284	290
Netherlands	18	55	121	212	269	283
UK	57	116	181	225	253	260
Japan	1	8	28	102	160	180

The UK comes surprisingly low on the list.

Colours: most popular
for Ford's British cars

The popularity of colour tends to be seasonal, so the list below shows the top three colours of each Ford model produced from August 1979 to March 1980.

Cortina
Of the 127 217 Cortinas produced:
1 Cordoba Beige – 15·5%
2 Corsican Blue – 12·7%
3 Venetian Red – 12·6%

Escort
Of the 95 149 Escorts produced:
1 Diamond White – 25·8%

2   Venetian Red – 12·7%
3   Cordoba Beige – 12·00%

Fiesta
Of the 51 219 Fiestas produced:
1   Venetian Red – 13·3%
2   Cordoba Beige – 12·8%
3   Diamond White – 11·00%

Capri
Of the 26 792 Capris produced:
1   Solar Gold – 18·7%
2   Venetian Red – 10·9%
3   Diamond White and Sirius Red – 9·9%

Granada
Of the 7 378 Granadas produced:
1   Solar Gold – 20·6%
2   Strato Silver – 14·5%
3   Sirius Red – 9·06%

COMMENT: Ford's new colour range for 1980 includes Cordoba Beige, Sirius Red, Java Green, Sable Brown and Solar Gold, shades which are apparently all subtly different from the previous colour range of Nevada Beige, Jupiter Red, Nova Green, Roman Bronze and Oyster Gold.

'Broadly speaking,' said a spokesman for Ford, 'some colours look attractive on certain models. A bright salmon pink might look agreeable on a Fiesta but on a Granada you might need sunglasses.

'With regard to a colour rising in popularity, I'd say that white is definitely an improving colour, but people go for brighter colours in winter and softer colours in summer.'

Cars and central heating, 1975

Estimated percentage of the total household population, region by region, which has a car and also central heating. Well, they both begin with C.

	one or more cars	central heating
UK total	56	47
North	51	52
Yorkshire and Humberside	51	42
East Midlands	57	50
East Anglia	71	55
South East except Greater London	67	57
Greater London	51	42
South West	67	53
West Midlands	58	45
North West	48	41
Wales	58	40
Scotland	45	43

CATCH PHRASES

Norman Vaughan made famous the catch words 'swinging' and 'dodgy' – ordinary words used in a slightly unusual way which caught the public imagination. Here are his own favourite catch phrases, listed in chronological order.

1 'Can you hear me, mother?' Sandy Powell
2 'I thang yew' Arthur Askey
3 'You've deaded me, you dirty rotten swine!' Peter Sellers as Bluebottle in *The Goon Show*
4 'I've arrived, and to prove it I'm here' Max Bygraves in his radio days

5 'I'm in charge'   Bruce Forsyth in *Sunday Night at the London Palladium*

6 'What do you think of it so far?'
  'Rubbish!'   Morecambe and Wise

7 'Just like that!'   Tommy Cooper

8 'It's goodnight from me . . .'
  '. . . and it's goodnight from him.'   The Two Ronnies

9 'Brill' and 'soopersonic'   Little and Large

10 'How tickled I ham'   Ken Dodd

CATHEDRALS

The most popular

In order, these are the most visited cathedrals in England based on attendance figures. The figures, which refer to 1977 and come from the English Tourist Board, are in many cases estimates. Westminster Abbey, the No 1, is not technically a cathedral, nor are King's College Chapel, Bath Abbey, Beverley Minster, Selby Abbey, Tewkesbury Abbey nor St George's Chapel, Windsor, but the ETB calls them 'greater churches' and lumps them with the 40 official cathedrals in their 1979 book on English cathedrals.

Westminster Abbey	3 million +
St Paul's, London	2 million +
Canterbury Cathedral	1 million +
York Minster	1 million +
King's College Chapel, Cambridge	1 million
St George's Chapel, Windsor	1 million
Coventry	666 000
Salisbury	500 000
Durham	500 000
Chester	450 000
Exeter	375 000
Lincoln	375 000

Norwich	375 000
Oxford	375 000
Wells	375 000
Winchester	375 000
Ely	300 000
Westminster RC	250 000
St Albans	250 000
Bath Abbey	250 000
Worcester	200 000
Chichester	200 000
Truro	200 000
Carlisle	150 000
Ripon	150 000
Hereford	100 000
Bury St Edmunds	100 000
Guildford	100 000
Lichfield	100 000
Peterborough	100 000
Rochester	100 000
Beverley Minster	75 000
Tewkesbury Abbey	60 000
Bristol	60 000
Liverpool C of E	60 000
Southwell	60 000
Southwark	50 000
Arundel RC	45 000
Sheffield	40 000
Manchester	40 000
Newcastle	30 000
Selby	30 000
Liverpool RC	25 000
Portsmouth	20 000
Leicester	8 000
Bradford	4 000

Reasons for visiting
a cathedral

In 1977, in a one-day poll, visitors to England's cathedrals were asked: 'which one of these statements best describes why you came to the cathedral today?'

	%
Particularly wanted to see this cathedral	66
It seemed a good idea to visit as I was in the area	13
Somewhere to go as a day out with family or friends	8
Filling in spare time	4
Particularly wanted to see a cathedral	3
Included in the tour I am on and tour chosen partly for cathedral visit	2
Included in the tour I am on but cathedral visit unimportant in choice of tour	2
None of these	1
Not known	1

CEREALS

In Europe, Britain eats most cereals, despite all the eggs and bacon. Continental breakfasts, as we all know, are no use for real men.

Consumption per annum of breakfast cereals in Europe, per household

Euromonitor, 1975

	pounds weight
UK	23·6
Netherlands	20·9

W. Germany	18·7
Austria	16·7
Sweden	8·6
France	8·4
Norway } Switzerland	8·1
Belgium	6·8
Denmark } Italy	5·07
Spain	4·2

The top ten cereals in Britain, 1979

1 Kellogg's Corn Flakes
2 Weetabix
3 Kellogg's All-Bran
4 Nabisco Shredded Wheat
5 Lyons' Ready Brek
6 Kellogg's Rice Krispies
7 Kellogg's Frosties
8 Quaker Sugar Puffs
9 Alpen (Weetabix Ltd)
10 Kellogg's 30% Bran Flakes

Kellogg's, the leading producer, turn out nearly $1\frac{1}{2}$ million packets of cereal every day. If the packed cartons were laid end to end, a day's output would reach from their Manchester plant to Dover, over 250 miles away. The cereal cartons used at Kellogg's account for 25 000 tons of board per year.

CHAMPAGNE

Euromonitor, 1977

Number of bottles of
champagne consumed annually

France is bound to win, as it's French champagne we're counting, but the UK doesn't do too badly, for a supposedly second-class country. Germany really ought to try harder.

	millions
France	124·5
UK	7·3
Italy	7·3
Belgium	6·8
USA	4·8
W. Germany	4·0
Switzerland	2·3

CHARITIES

UK charities, 1977–8,
which receive annually over
£4 million in income

Social Trends

	income £ thousands
Dr Barnardo's	13 994
Spastics Society	11 479
Imperial Cancer Research Fund	9 400
Royal National Institute for the Blind	9 119
Oxfam	7 676

Royal National Lifeboat Institution	7 052
Save the Children Fund	6 406
Help the Aged	6 212
Christian Aid	4 694
RSPCA	4 525

In 1979, there were 126 000 charities registered with the Charity Commissioners and the total income was just under £2 000 million.

CHOCOLATES

In a recent survey carried out by Cadbury's they analysed the popularity of their milk and plain chocolate centres – trying to discover which centres in a box were eaten first.

Cadbury's most popular
chocolate centres

1 Hazel Whirl – milk chocolate
2 Noisette Whirl – milk chocolate
3 Caramel – milk or plain chocolate
4 Whole Brazil dipped in plain chocolate

The following six centres are also very popular, but are in no particular order of preference.

1 Hazelnut in soft toffee – milk chocolate
2 Coffee Creme – milk or plain chocolate
3 Hazel Cluster – plain chocolate
4 Fudge – milk or plain chocolate

5 Montelimar – plain chocolate
6 Cherry Creme – plain chocolate

As a general rule, hard, nutty centres are more popular than soft, gooey centres.

CHRISTIAN NAMES

Despite the absence of *The Times* for ten months of 1979, the indefatigable Margaret Brown of York analysed the births announcements and provided her list for *The Times* correspondence column.

Top people's names, 1979

For the sixteenth year in succession, James was the name most frequently chosen by readers announcing the birth of their sons in *The Times*. As in the previous four years, Elizabeth led the table for girls.

(The figures in parentheses indicate the position held in 1978.)

	boys		girls	
1	James	61 (1)	Elizabeth	32 (1)
2	Edward	36 (2)	Sarah	20 (6)
3	Thomas	27 (5)	Jane	18 (3)
4	Nicholas	26 (10)	Victoria	18 (5)
5	John	24 (6)	Mary	16 (4)
6	Alexander	21 (3)	Caroline	15 (14)
7	William	21 (4)	Clare	15 (12)
8	Charles	18 (7)	Louise	15 (2)
9	David	16 (9)	Helen	11 (10)
10	Richard	16 (8)	Anna	11 (22)

Even though only seven weeks' material was available for 1979, the same ten boys' names headed the list as in 1978.

Most popular names in a
London suburb, 1979

Meanwhile, down in London SW15, these are the most fre-
quently chosen names in a suburban maternity hospital –
Queen Mary's, Roehampton – as noted in 1979 by Jane Milne,
who photographed new-born babies for a firm called Cradle
Pictures. The list tallies remarkably well with the Top
People's List.

boys		girls	
James	13	Claire	13
Daniel	} 8	Nicola	12
Thomas		Emma	8
Richard	7	Kate (Katie)	7
Adam		Catherine	
Alexander		Joanna	} 6
Paul	} 6	Michelle	
Simon		Anna	
Benjamin		Sarah	} 5
Christopher		Victoria	
Darren		Elizabeth	
David		Jodie	} 4
Lee		Natasha	
Matthew	} 5	Caroline	
Nicholas		Helen	
Oliver		Julia	
Peter		Laura	
Robert		Louise	} 3
Edward	} 4	Lucy	
Stephen		Melissa	
		Rachel	
		Samantha	

CLASS

The most middle-class places

These are the local education areas of England and Wales with the highest percentage of the population in the non-manual class.

Bromley	63·1
Kingston-upon-Thames	62·6
Barnet	61·8
Richmond-upon-Thames	61·4
Harrow	61·4
Surrey (as a whole)	58·5
Sutton	58·4
Isle of Wight	57·7
Croydon	56·9
Redbridge	55·3

The most working-class places

The areas with the lowest percentage of non-manual workers.

Barnsley	22·4
Sandwell	23·4
Doncaster	25·9
Knowsley	26·6
Barking	26·6
Sunderland	26·8
Rotherham	27·0
Mid-Glamorgan	27·5
Newham, London	27·9
Wakefield	28·0

Class: in the Services

Commissioned officers in the armed services categorized by their school of origin. The Army chaps are certainly tops.

RAF	State schools	74%
	Public schools	17%
	Overseas	1%
	Rest	8%
Army	Public schools	55%
	State schools	41%
	Rest	4%
Royal Navy	State schools	62%
	Public schools	28%
	Rest	10%

Jilly Cooper's lower-class words to avoid

Jilly Cooper, the well-known writer, beauty and lady of impeccable taste, has graciously given us a list of eleven words which you should not use, unless you want to be seen, or heard, to be lower class. In brackets, she gives the correct upper-class usage.

Wellies (gum boots)
Blouse (shirt)
Sweater (jersey)
Blazer (boating jacket)
Place a bet (Have a bet, or simply, bet)
Ice-skating (skating)
Fresh fruit (fruit)
Go on holiday (go away, or go to a specific country, such as go to France, go to Switzerland)
Periods (the curse)
Pregnant (having a baby)
Penis (cock)

Mrs Cooper adds that the various words for WC are no longer a reliable class indicator. 'Lavatory' was the upper-class word, but now the middle classes use it, having forsaken 'loo'. 'Toilet', the lower-class term, is being replaced by 'loo' amongst the lower classes. Meanwhile, 'toilet' is being used by the upper classes, originally satirically, in inverted commas, but now seriously. It's not easy, you see, being class conscious.

CLICHÉS

Below is the top 20 of over 450 clichés heard on radio and TV current affairs programmes (broadcasters, journalists and spokesmen only) over a period of one month (September 1979), and recorded exclusively for us by Mr Geoff Worrall of South Croydon, Surrey. Thanks, Geoff.

1 In (actual) fact
2 Situation
3 Industrial action
4 Viable
5 (De) escalation
6 Literally
7 Get into perspective
8 Democratically elected
9 In the light of
10 In a nutshell
11 Free collective bargaining
12 Not what you would call
13 Negotiating table
14 On the cards
15 Bread and butter issues
16 Crux of the matter
17 Can I just make this point
18 Grass roots
19 Scenario
20 Lame duck

CONSERVATION

The spending tabled here covers local authority conservation measures, including expenditure on tree preservation and tree planting. Grants given and received by the local authority for works in conservation areas or on listed buildings are included.

The top ten spenders – £ per 1 000 population

1	Camden (London)	2 165
2	Bath	1 582
3	South Tyneside	1 412
4	Norwich	1 396
5	Easington	1 370
6	Chester	1 169
7	Penwith	1 142
8	Lambeth (London)	1 044
9	North Kesteven	1 090
10	Canterbury	1 001

COUNTIES

Acreage of English counties

This also gives you an extra list for the price of one – a list of all the English counties with their correct names. (For counties by population density, see 'P' for Population.)

Yorkshire, North	2 053 126
Cumbria	1 682 239
Devonshire	1 658 285

Lincolnshire	1 454 351
Norfolk	1 323 371
Northumberland	1 243 692
Hereford and Worcestershire	970 203
Suffolk	940 800
Hampshire	934 474
Kent	922 196
Essex	907 850
Cornwall	876 295
Humberside	867 784
Shropshire	862 479
Wiltshire	860 109
Somerset	852 434
Cambridgeshire	842 433
Lancashire	751 063
Staffordshire	671 184
Dorset	655 818
Gloucestershire	652 741
Derbyshire	650 146
Oxfordshire	645 314
Leicestershire	630 842
Durham	601 939
Northamptonshire	584 970
Cheshire	575 375
Nottinghamshire	534 735
Yorkshire, West	503 863
Sussex, West	498 178
Warwickshire	489 405
Buckinghamshire	465 019
Sussex, East	443 634
Surrey	414 922
Hertfordshire	403 787
Greater London	390 302
Yorkshire, South	385 605
Avon	332 596
Greater Manchester	317 285
Berkshire	310 178
Bedfordshire	305 026
West Midlands	222 258

Merseyside	159 750
Cleveland	144 086
Tyne and Wear	133 390
Isle of Wight	94 134

CRICKET

All our cricket lists have been painstakingly collected by Nicholas Mason, Deputy Sports Editor of *The Sunday Times*. Well played, Nick.

All-round performance at
Test Match level

Players who have scored 1 000 runs and taken 100 wickets in Tests for England (figures correct to May 1980).

player	tests	runs	wickets	test in which double was achieved
I. T. Botham	25	1336	139	21st
M. W. Tate	39	1198	155	33rd
A. W. Greig	58	3599	141	37th
F. J. Titmus	53	1449	153	40th
W. Rhodes	58	2325	127	44th
T. E. Bailey	61	2290	132	47th
R. Illingworth	61	1836	122	47th

Full list of hat-tricks

(three wickets in consecutive balls) taken in
Test Matches for England

W. BATES v Australia (Melbourne, 1882–3)
J. BRIGGS v Australia (Sydney, 1891–2)
G. A. LOHMANN v South Africa (Port Elizabeth, 1895–6)
J. T. HEARNE v Australia (Leeds, 1899)
M. J. C. ALLOM v New Zealand (Christchurch, 1929–30)
T. W. J. GODDARD v South Africa (Johannesburg, 1938–9)
P. J. LOADER v West Indies (Leeds, 1957)

Highest total for each of
the first-class counties

Derbyshire	645	v Hampshire (Derby, 1898)
Essex	692	v Somerset (Taunton, 1895)
Glamorgan	587 (8 wkts)	v Derbyshire (Cardiff, 1951)
Gloucestershire	653 (6 wkts)	v Glamorgan (Bristol, 1928)
Hampshire	672 (7 wkts)	v Somerset (Taunton, 1899)
Kent	803 (4 wkts)	v Essex (Brentwood, 1934)
Lancashire	801	v Somerset (Taunton, 1895)
Leicestershire	701 (4 wkts)	v Worcestershire (Worcester, 1906)
Middlesex	642 (3 wkts)	v Hampshire (Southampton, 1923)
Northamptonshire	557 (6 wkts)	v Sussex (Hove, 1914)
Nottinghamshire	739 (7 wkts)	v Leicestershire (Nottingham, 1903)
Somerset	675 (9 wkts)	v Hampshire (Bath, 1924)
Surrey	811	v Somerset (Oval, 1899)
Sussex	705 (8 wkts)	v Surrey (Hastings, 1902)
Warwickshire	657 (6 wkts)	v Hampshire (Birmingham, 1899)
Worcestershire	633	v Warwickshire (Worcester, 1906)
Yorkshire	887	v Warwickshire (Birmingham, 1896)

Lowest total by each
first-class county

Derbyshire	16	v Nottinghamshire (Nottingham, 1879)
Essex	30	v Yorkshire (Leyton, 1901)
Glamorgan	22	v Lancashire (Liverpool, 1924)
Gloucestershire	17	v Australia (Cheltenham, 1896)
Hampshire	15	v Warwickshire (Birmingham, 1922)
Kent	18	v Sussex (Gravesend, 1867)
Lancashire	25	v Derbyshire (Manchester, 1871)
Leicestershire	25	v Kent (Leicester, 1912)
Middlesex	20	v MCC (Lord's, 1864)
Northamptonshire	12	v Gloucestershire (Gloucester, 1907)
Nottinghamshire	13	v Yorkshire (Nottingham, 1901)
Somerset	25	v Gloucestershire (Bristol, 1947)
Surrey	16	v Nottinghamshire (Oval, 1880)
Sussex	19	v Nottinghamshire (Hove, 1873)
Warwickshire	16	v Kent (Tonbridge, 1913)
Worcestershire	24	v Yorkshire (Huddersfield, 1903)
Yorkshire	23	v Hampshire (Middlesbrough, 1965)

A full list of the success
records of all the players
who have captained England
in Test Matches since
the war

[Up until May, 1980]

The Wisden Book of Test Cricket

name	won	lost	drawn	
W. R. Hammond	1	3	5	(pre-war: 3 – 0 – 8)
N. W. D. Yardley	4	7	3	
K. Cranston	0	0	1	
F. G. Mann	2	0	5	
F. R. Brown	5	6	4	
N. D. Howard	1	0	3	
D. B. Carr	0	1	0	
L. Hutton	11	4	8	

D. S. Sheppard	1	0	1
P. B. H. May	20	10	11
M. C. Cowdrey	8	4	15
E. R. Dexter	9	7	14
M. J. K. Smith	5	3	17
D. B. Close	6	0	1
T. W. Graveney	0	0	1
R. Illingworth	12	5	14
A. R. Lewis	1	2	5
M. H. Denness	6	5	8
J. H. Edrich	0	1	0
A. W. Greig	3	5	6
J. M. Brearley	15	4	7
G. Boycott	1	1	2

Oldest players to represent England in a Test Match

(Age shown on final day of their last Test Match)

52 years 165 days – W. RHODES (v West Indies, 1929–30)
50 years 320 days – W. G. GRACE (v Australia, 1899)
50 years 303 days – G. GUNN (v West Indies, 1929–30)
49 years 139 days – J. SOUTHERTON (v Australia, 1876–7)*
47 years 249 days – J. B. HOBBS (v Australia, 1930)
47 years 87 days – F. E. WOOLLEY (v Australia, 1934)
46 years 202 days – H. STRUDWICK (v Australia, 1926)
46 years 41 days – E. HENDREN (v West Indies, 1934–5)
45 years 245 days – G. O. B. ALLEN (v West Indies, 1947–8)
45 years 215 days – P. HOLMES (v India, 1932)
45 years 140 days – D. B. CLOSE (v West Indies, 1976)

*This was also Southerton's Test debut

CRIME

Since the 1950s there has been a substantial increase in crime figures. Whether there are *more* criminals is not exactly known. It might just be the same proportion of criminals committing more crimes each.

Offences 'cleared up' is the police term. It does not necessarily mean successful convictions – it includes those cautioned or sentenced for other offences.

Serious offences recorded by the police

Home Office figures for England and Wales

		thousands	
		1972	1978
1	Theft and handling stolen goods	1 009·5	1 441·3
2	Burglary	438·7	565·7
3	Criminal damage	41·9	306·2
4	Fraud and forgery	108·4	122·2
5	Violence against the person	52·4	87·1
6	Sexual offences	23·5	22·4
7	Robbery	8·9	13·1
8	Other offences	6·9	3·5
	Total serious offences	1690·2	2 561·5
	Serious offences cleared up (percentages)	45·8	41·5

Non-indictable offences – total 1976

	thousands
Motoring offences	1 211
Other offences	173
Drunkenness	103
Motor vehicle licences	102
Wireless & Telegraphy Acts	35
Assault	12

CRISPS

Just in case you get peckish, reading all those cricket lists, here's something completely different.

Britain is a big crisp-munching nation: forty packs of crisps for every man, woman and child are eaten each year. The largest consumers of crisps are the Americans, but we run a close second in an international list of seven.

A spokesman for Smiths' Crisps says: 'Constant research is being carried out to find new flavours that people will want. We recently tried curried crisps but the public didn't take to them at all. Four years ago we re-introduced the old plain crisps with the little blue pack of salt (Salt 'n' Shake) and these are immensely popular. So are square crisps, made from reconstituted potato, but at the moment they are not available throughout the country.'

The ten most popular flavours of crisps in Britain

1 Ready Salted
2 Cheese & Onion
3 Salt & Vinegar
4 Salt 'n' Shake
5 Bovril
6 Beef
7 Smoky Bacon
8 Gammon
9 Chicken
10 Tomato Sauce

The ten most popular
proprietary savoury snacks

1 Monster Munch
2 Quavers
3 Country Crunch
4 Outer Spacers
5 Wotsits
6 Frazzles
7 Football Crazy
8 Chipsticks
9 Horror Bags
10 Hula Hoops

DATING

An American term, but in Britain there are several computer dating firms and one of them, Dateline International, went through their records and compiled this list for us.

The average Dateline member

female
is single
is Central or Northern European in colouring
is 5ft to 5ft 4in in height
is of medium build
never smokes
occasionally drinks
Protestant (C of E)
not interested in politics
between 26 and 35 years old

male
is single
is Central or Northern European in colouring
is 5ft 9in to 6ft in height
is of medium build
never smokes
occasionally drinks
Protestant (C of E)
not interested in politics
between 26 and 35 years old

she wants a man who is	*he wants a woman who is*
single or divorced	single
Central or Northern	doesn't mind, but slight
European but does not mind	preference for central or
Southern European or Latin	Northern European – not
	Asian or negroid
not less than 5ft 6in but	he doesn't mind what height
prefers him to be at least	she is but is keen on girls
5ft 9in or over	over 5ft 6in
she does not mind what build	he definitely does not want
he is	her to be fat
she would prefer him not to	he does not care if she
smoke but does not mind	smokes or not
the occasional	
cigarette	
she prefers a moderate	he prefers a moderate
drinker	drinker
she doesn't mind what his	he doesn't mind at all about
religion is but would prefer	her religion
him not to be Jewish	
she doesn't mind if he is	he would like her not to be
interested in politics or not	interested in politics at all,
or what his politics are	and certainly does not want
	her to be left wing

DEATHS

In the UK
analysis by cause, 1976

Males	*thousands*
Deaths from natural causes	327·7
Coronary disease, angina	103·2
Other natural causes	60·5

Respiratory diseases	54·4
Cancer (except lung cancer)	46·0
Cerebrovascular diseases	33·5
Cancer of the lung	30·1
Accidents	5·6
Transport accidents	5·3
Suicide	2·6
Homicide and war	0·7

females

Deaths from natural causes	328·1
Other natural causes	79·2
Coronary disease, angina	78·9
Cancer (except lung cancer)	57·8
Cerebrovascular diseases	54·1
Respiratory diseases	50·2
Cancer of the lung	7·9
Accidents	6·3
Transport accidents	2·3
Suicide	1·7
Homicide and war	0·4
Pregnancy, childbirth, abortion	0·1

Deaths from accidents in the home in GB, 1977

Social Trends

Falls remain the most common cause of death from accidents in the home. Old people, and especially older women, are most at risk.

	males aged:					
	0–4	*5–14*	*15–44*	*45–64*	*65 & over*	*all ages*
accident type						
Falls	17	6	69	158	565	815
Fires	29	27	46	66	134	302
Poisoning	10	3	163	112	53	341
Other	26	10	47	48	57	188

| Suffocation | 83 | 16 | 84 | 67 | 36 | 286 |
| All accidents | 165 | 62 | 409 | 451 | 845 | 1932 |

	females aged:					
	0–4	*5–14*	*15–44*	*45–64*	*65 &* *over*	*all* *ages*
accident type						
Falls	12	1	25	122	1689	1849
Fires	32	26	40	56	238	392
Poisoning	6	8	117	138	84	353
Other	29	4	21	36	173	263
Suffocation	63	3	25	41	42	174
All accidents	142	42	228	393	2226	3031

Percentage of total deaths caused by diseases of the respiratory system

World Health Organization

	%
UK	13·3
Ireland	13·1
Spain	11·9
Norway	9·1
Japan	7·7
Australia	7·6
Italy	7·4
Austria	7·0
Denmark	6·9
France	6·6
Belgium ⎫ Canada ⎭	6·5
Netherlands	6·4
W. Germany ⎫ Switzerland ⎭	5·9
USA	5·6
Sweden	4·2

DISEASES

Notifications of certain
infectious diseases in the UK, 1975

	number
Measles	158 572
Food poisoning	10 301
Scarlet fever	10 235
Tuberculosis – respiratory	9 579
Whooping cough	9 923
Dysentery	9 375
Tuberculosis – non-respiratory	2 955
Typhoid and paratyphoid fevers	301
Dyphtheria	12
Acute poliomyelitis	4

Smallpox, which had 62 cases in 1966, had completely
died out in the UK by 1975.

DOCTORS

Doctors of medicine who
became famous in other spheres

Somerset Maugham – writer
A. J. Cronin – writer
Hawley Harvey Crippen – murderer
Lord Hill – politician
Jonathan Miller – director
Richard Gordon – humorist
David Owen – politician
Dannie Abse – poet

DOGS

Most popular dogs' names

There are an estimated 6 million dogs in Britain: 500 000 of
them in London. The National Canine Defence League have
compiled the following information from the most popular
selling dog identity discs which they supply to their members.
The ten most popular dogs' names are:

1 Shep	6 Rover
2 Brandy	7 Skipper
3 Whisky	8 Prince
4 Patch	9 Rex
5 Butch	10 Lassie

The top five names that bitches are christened with are:

1 Sheba	4 Mandy
2 Sally	5 Tessa
3 Rosie	

Modern names: although not as popular as the old favourites
like Shep and Rex, there is a growing trend towards fancier
names such as Benji and Binnie. There's also a fad for Samson,
Nelson and Mishka. The latter is Russian for bear and is very
popular among the bigger breeds.

Cruft's Dog Show

The first dog show was held at Newcastle-upon-Tyne in 1859
but Cruft's was not started until 1886. This famous national
dog show now enjoys an international reputation. Before 1928
there was no award for Best-in-Show.

Best-in-Show winners

1928	Greyhound, 'Primely Sceptre'
1929	Scottish Terrier, 'Heather Necessity'
1930	Spaniel (Cocker), 'Luckystar of Ware'
1931	Spaniel (Cocker), 'Luckystar of Ware'
1932	Retriever (Labrador), 'Bramshaw Bob'
1933	Retriever (Labrador), 'Bramshaw Bob'
1934	Greyhound, 'Southball Moonstone'
1935	Pointer, 'Pennine Prima Donna'
1936	Chow Chow, Ch. 'Choonam Hung Kwong'
1937	Retriever (Labrador), Ch. 'Cheveralla Ben of Banchory'
1938	Spaniel (Cocker), 'Exquisite Model of Ware'
1939	Spaniel (Cocker), 'Exquisite Model of Ware'
1948	Spaniel (Cocker), 'Tracey Witch of Ware'
1950	Spaniel (Cocker), 'Tracey Witch of Ware'
1951	Welsh Terrier, 'Twynstar Dyma-Fi'
1952	Bulldog, Ch. 'Noways Chuckles'
1953	Great Dane, Ch. 'Elch Elder of Ouborough'
1954	(cancelled)
1955	Poodle (Standard), Ch. 'Tzigane Aggri of Nashend'
1956	Greyhound, 'Treetops Golden Falcon'
1957	Keeshond, Ch. 'Volkrijk of Vorden'
1958	Pointer, Ch. 'Chiming Bells'
1959	Welsh Terrier, Ch. 'Sandstorm Saracen'
1960	Irish Wolfhound, 'Sulhamstead Merman'
1961	Airedale Terrier, Ch. 'Riverina Tweedsbairn'
1962	Fox Terrier (Wire), Ch. 'Crackwyn Cockspur'
1963	Lakeland Terrier, 'Rogerholm Recruit'
1964	English Setter, Ch. 'Silbury Soames of Madavale'
1965	Alsatian (GSD), Ch. 'Fenton of Kentwood'
1966	Poodle (Toy), 'Oakington Puckshill Amber Sunblush'
1967	Lakeland Terrier, Ch. 'Stingray of Derryabah'
1968	Dalmatian, Ch. 'Fanhill Faune'
1969	Alsatian (GSD), Ch. 'Hendrawen's Nibelung of Charavigne'
1970	Pyrenean Mountain Dog, 'Bergerie Knur'

1971	Alsatian (GSD), Ch. 'Ramacon Swashbuckler'
1972	Bull Terrier, Ch. 'Abraxas Audacity'
1973	Cavalier King Charles Spaniel, 'Alansmere Aquarius'
1974	St Bernard, Ch. 'Burtonswood Bossy Boots'
1975	Fox Terrier (Wire), Ch. 'Brookewire Brandy of Layven'
1976	West Highland White Terrier, Ch. 'Dianthus Buttons'
1977	English Setter, 'Bournehouse Dancing Master'
1978	Fox Terrier (Wire), Ch. 'Harrowhill Huntsman'
1979	Kerry Blue Terrier, Ch. 'Callaghan of Leander'
1980	Black-haired Retriever, 'Shargleam Blackcap'

The 1980 Cruft's Show, the 84th, had 9 103 dogs on show worth around £5 million. There were 118 judges looking at 144 different breeds. The largest entries were of Afghans, Alsatians, Labradors and Golden Retrievers. The Supreme Champion Dog was expected to earn up to £50 000 in breeding and advertising fees.

DOUBLE ACTS

In the considered opinion of Little and Large, two gentlemen who appear together, this is their competition.

Little and Large's
top ten double acts

1 Morecambe and Wise
2 The Two Ronnies
3 Cannon and Ball
4 Rod Hull and Emu
5 Steptoe and Son

6 George and Mildred
7 Windsor Davies and Don Estelle
8 Ronnie Dukes and Ricki Lee
9 Sooty and Sweep
10 Hinge and Bracket

DREAMS

The ten most common dreams

Compiled by Nerys Dee, dream interpreter for *Prediction* magazine, who kindly explains what they stand for.

1 Houses: the whole self – these are the mansions of the soul. Attics are places in our minds where we keep half-forgotten high hopes; basements, on the other hand, are the cellars of our minds where dark shadows often lurk.

2 Water: emotions and feelings. Depending on depth, clarity or on swiftness, various comparisons can be drawn.

3 Aeroplanes: high ideals. When not a reflection of the fear of flying they indicate high-flying ambitions which probably need bringing down to earth.

4 Snakes: energy, ranging from basic sexual desires to energy for healing, as seen by the symbol of the medical profession which incorporates two snakes twining round a stick.

5 Doors: opportunities. Literally, they mean new openings in life linked with surprises.

6 Eyes: foresight. These are the windows of the soul, showing problems in a new perspective.

7 A tower: a warning, especially about towering ambitions. The higher we climb the further we fall.

8 A tree: family, or something to do with family. It indicates the family tree, with all its branches, roots and relationships. Seeing trees uprooted means something in the family has gone wrong.

9 Teeth: a change. Dreaming of loose teeth or lost teeth signifies a change in health for the better.
10 Mountains: desire, especially the peak of desire often associated with the hope of sexual conquest.

COMMENT: Most dreams are symbolic. They are messages from ourselves to ourselves. Says Nerys Dee, 'Our dreaming, scheming minds love to use stand-ins or symbols. Much of their symbolism comes from the everyday language we use. For example, a pig in a dream usually represents someone whom we know pretty well. And why not? From schooldays we've used that expression as an all too apt description of someone!'

Nerys maintains that interpreting dreams is not as difficult as it seems. She says, 'One should always look for the literal interpretations; and simple explanations before searching for hidden symbols. Literal dreams are action replays showing us things we have missed with our conscious minds. A lady wrote to me saying she had had a dream about her kitchen; all her plants were wilting on the window ledge and there was a nasty smell. I wrote back telling her she could possibly have a gas leak, so she called the Gas Board and indeed, they discovered a serious gas leak. Her conscious sense of smell had not detected it but her subconscious mind had. When people dream of car accidents it is not always a premonition. I tell them to check the car, the brakes or something else might need fixing.'

DUKES

Non-royal British dukes in order of the year of their original creation. Now you know all Dukes. Don't get them mixed up with dogs or dreams.

Norfolk	1483
Somerset	1547
Hamilton	1643

Buccleuch	1663
Grafton	1675
Richmond	1675
Beaufort	1682
St Albans	1684
Bedford	1694
Devonshire	1694
Argyll	1701
Marlborough	1702
Atholl	1703
Rutland	1703
Montrose	1707
Roxburghe	1707
Portland	1716
Manchester	1719
Newcastle (under Lyme)	1756
Leinster	1766
Northumberland	1766
Wellington	1814
Sutherland	1833
Abercorn	1868
Westminster	1874
Fife	1900

The four royal dukes are:

Duke of Cornwall (Prince Charles)	1337
Duke of Gloucester	1928
Duke of Kent	1934
Duke of Edinburgh (Prince Philip)	1947

EATING

Egon Ronay's favourite people
to eat dinner with

Mr Ronay, the well-known arbiter and guide to what to eat and where, has chosen the people he would most like to dine with. Some are living, some are dead, but each, so he thinks, would bring to the table something in the way of expertise, wisdom or wit.

1 **Dr Johnson** Everyone would want to have dinner with him, for his love of food and his love of conversation.

2 **Talleyrand** The great French diplomat's greatest attraction would have been his chef, Câreme, the most magnificent chef in the whole of France at that time.

3 **Nubar Gilbenkian** People now think he was simply a very greedy person. He wasn't. He had the most awesome knowledge of food and drink.

4 **John Apple** I'm now thinking of present-day people, friends with whom I love to dine. John Apple is head of the *New York Times* bureau in London and combines great knowledge of food with a great sense of humour.

5 **Kenneth Lo** He's the leading expert on Chinese cookery in Britain. He's also very good on tennis – I love talking about tennis when I'm eating. Kenneth was a Cambridge tennis blue.

6 **Sir Alexander Glen** Sandy used to be chairman of the British Tourist Authority. He's the nicest man I know, and loves his food and drink.

7 **Mario Cassandro** He's the Mario of Mario and Franco. He has the boldness of the self-made man and an utter lack of respect for the Establishment. So he's always great company.

8 **Charles Wintour** Editor of the *Evening Standard*. I love talking politics with someone who knows a lot. I know very little, so I like listening.

9 **Michel Guérard** He's probably the greatest French chef

of today, the creator of *cuisine minceur*. He has a sense of art in everything he does.

10 **Peter Ustinov** I've never met him, but if I had to choose someone for his conversation, he does seem to be the best living conversationalist.

No women, Mr Ronay? Rather sexist, don't you think? Surely there are some ladies somewhere you would like to dine with? 'Yes, well, in that case Elizabeth David. I've never met her but it would be nice to do so. Of course, most of all I'd like to meet M. F. K. Fisher, whom I've never met either. She's a lady in her seventies who lives in America. She's fantastic, the best writer on gastronomy in the world today.'

EDUCATION

Smallest primary school classes

These are the local education authorities in England and Wales where the pupil-teacher ratio is under 20 to 1. So if you want a small class for your child, you know where to move.

Inner London	15·1
Dyfed	17·3
Powys	17·7
Brent	17·7
Haringey	18·2
Newham	18·5
Wolverhampton	19·1
Ealing	19·2
Newcastle	19·8
Manchester	19·9
Gwynedd	19·9

Largest primary school classes

Tameside	24·0
Bromley	24·1
Bolton	24·1
Hampshire	24·2
Bexley	24·4
Somerset	24·5
Oxfordshire	24·6
Hereford & Worcester	24·6
Wirral	24·7
Avon	24·7
Dudley	25·7
Stockport	26·7

Highest expenditure per pupil on primary schools

Highest expenditure per pupil in primary schools, 1980, based on the capitation allowances (expenditure on books, equipment, stationery).

Inner London	£ 25·39
Brent	24·84
Haringey	21·94
Waltham Forest	21·32
Harrow	20·08
Bromley	19·53
Ealing	19·57
South Tyneside	19·34

Lowest expenditure per pupil in primary schools

Gwynedd	£ 10·97
Hereford & Worcester	10·90
Lancashire	10·88
Leicestershire	10·27
Sefton	10·26
Leeds	10·22
Bradford	10·08
West Sussex	10·03

ELECTRICITY

In an all-electric house, the average British family of four consumes almost 19 000 units of electricity a year. This is where it goes.

Electricity consumed
– units per year per household

Central heating	10 000
Heating water	3 500
Cooker	2 000
Dishwasher	850
Washing machine	270
Deep freeze	900
Colour TV	500
Fridge	325
Electric kettle	250
Lighting	200
Electric iron	75
Vacuum cleaner	30
Toaster	20
	18 920

EMPLOYMENT

The number of employees in
each industry group in the UK, 1976

	thousands
Total number of employees in employment	22 491·4
1 Manufacturing	7 290·1
2 Professional and scientific services	3 621·3
3 Distributive trades	2 708·2
4 Transport and communication	1 484·7
5 Miscellaneous services (excluding hotels, restaurants, etc.)	1 398·5
6 Construction	1 271·2
7 Insurance, banking, finance and business services	1 109·8
8 Local government service	1 030·5
9 Hotels, restaurants, public houses, clubs, catering contractors	825·7
10 National government service	670·4
11 Agriculture, forestry, fishing	392·9
12 Mining and quarrying	344·4
13 Gas, electricity and water	343·7

In 1978, according to the Government's *Social Trends*, the total labour force had risen to 25 million – divided under five broad headings:
 1 Private sector – 15·6 million
 2 Local authority – 3·0 million
 3 Central government (including HM Forces) – 2·3 million
 4 Public corporations – 2·1 million
 5 Self-employed – 1·9 million

The number of employees in each manufacturing industry in the UK, 1976

The biggest single employer comes under the heading 'Manufacturing' where the total employees comes to 7 290 000. This is how it breaks down:

		thousands
1	Mechanical engineering	930·3
2	Electrical engineering	744·8
3	Vehicles	735·4
4	Food, drink and tobacco	718·3
5	Paper, printing and publishing	542·2
6	Metal goods not elsewhere specified	529·6
7	Textiles	521·8
8	Metal manufacture	473·7
9	Chemicals and allied industries	425·8
10	Clothing and footwear	395·3
11	Other manufacturing industries	331·2
12	Bricks, pottery, glass, cement etc.	267·0
13	Timber, furniture etc.	264·3
14	Shipbuilding and marine engineering	181·7
15	Instrument engineering	148·0
16	Leather, leather goods and fur	42·2
17	Coal and petroleum products	38·4

Civil Service staff, UK, 1977

analysis by ministerial responsibility

		thousands
1	Ministry of Defence*	258·7
2	Social Services	98·3
3	Inland Revenue	83·9
4	Environment	61·5

5	Employment	52·5
6	Home	32·6
7	Customs and Excise	29·3
8	Agriculture, Fisheries and Food	15·5
9	Transport	13·6
10	Foreign and Commonwealth	12·4
11	Department for National Savings	12·2
12	Industry	9·7
13	Trade	9·7
14	Education and Science	4·0
15	Treasury	3·9
16	Energy	1·3
17	Prices and Consumer Protection	0·4
	Other civil departments	46·1
	Total: civil and defence departments	745·6

*Ministry of Defence does not include HM Forces

EPITAPHS

A Fine and Private Place
by Joan Bakewell, John Drummond and Andrew Lawson

After all those figures, now some words. These epitaphs, culled from gravestones in various parts of the country, are worth remembering for their wisdom or wit.

> Death is a fisherman; the world we see
> A fish pond is, and we the fishes be;
> He sometimes angles, like doth with us play,
> And slily takes us one by one away.
>
> High Wycombe, Buckinghamshire

Jean Anderson, died 1770
> Praises on Tombs are vainly spent:
> A good Name is a Monument.
>
> Hammersmith, London

Here lyes the bodeys of George Young
and Isabel Guthrie, and all their posterity
for fifty years backwards. November 1757.
                              Montrose, Angus

John Geddes, died 1689
    This world is a city
    full of streets, and
    Death the merchant
    that all men meets.
    If life were a thing
    that money could buy,
    The poor could not live
    and the rich
    would not die.
                Elgin Cathedral, Moray

Elizabeth Ireland, died 1779
    Here I lie, at the chancel door,
    Here I lie because I'm poor.
    The farther in, the more you pay;
    Here lie I as warm as they.
                        Ashburton, Devon

Mary Broomfield, died 1755, aged eighty
    The chief concern of her life for the last
    twenty-five years was to order and provide
    for her funeral. Her greatest pleasure
    was to think and talk about it. She lived
    many years on a pension of 9d per week,
    and yet she saved £5, which at her own
    request was laid out on her funeral.
                        Macclesfield, Cheshire

58

Erected to the memory of John MacFarlane, drowned in the waters of the Leith by a few affectionate friends

Thomas Crabtree, died 1680, aged nineteen
    Short was my Stay in this vain World,
    All but a seeming Laughter;
    Therefore mark well thy Words and Ways,
    For thou com'st posting after.
St Peter's, Leeds, West Yorkshire

EXPENDITURE

Public expenditure

	£ million at 1978–9
Social Security	15 441
Defence, overseas aid, and other overseas services	9 251
Health and personal social services	8 980
Education	8 702
Housing	4 923
Environmental services	3 293
Other expenditure on programmes	2 852
Trade, industry, agriculture, fisheries, food and forestry: less food subsidies	2 765
Roads and transport	2 958
Law, order and protective services	2 260
Northern Ireland	2 196
Libraries, museums and the arts	387
Food subsidies	73

Consumer expenditure

Percentages of total consumers' expenditure at current prices

	1951	1961	1966	1971	1972	1973	1974	1975	1976	1977	1978
Food	29·8	24·5	22·0	19·8	18·6	18·7	18·8	19·0	19·1	19·3	18·7
Housing	8·7	9·9	11·8	13·0	13·2	13·8	14·2	14·6	14·4	14·8	14·4
Transport and vehicles	5·9	9·1	10·6	12·6	12·9	12·4	11·7	12·2	12·5	12·5	13·0
Alcohol	7·6	6·0	6·7	7·3	7·3	7·5	7·5	7·6	7·9	7·8	7·8
Clothing and footwear	11·0	9·7	8·9	8·4	8·4	8·5	8·6	8·1	7·8	7·6	7·7
Fuel and light	3·9	4·5	4·8	4·6	4·5	4·2	4·4	4·6	4·9	5·1	4·8
Durable household goods	4·7	4·8	4·3	4·6	5·2	5·3	5·1	5·0	5·0	4·8	4·9
Tobacco	7·9	6·8	6·2	4·8	4·5	4·3	4·3	4·3	4·2	4·3	4·1
Other goods, services, and miscellaneous	20·5	24·7	24·7	24·9	25·4	25·3	25·4	24·6	24·2	23·8	24·6

FANCY DRESS

Berman's, the London Costumiers

The most popular fancy dress costumes in the UK are:

Men
1 Roman
2 Futuristic, space
3 Cavalier
4 Cowboys and Indians
5 Elizabethan and Tudor
6 Roarin' Twenties
7 Comic strip characters: Superman, Batman, Robin
8 Sea monsters
9 Military uniforms
10 Famous people: Henry VIII, Robinson Crusoe,
Davy Crockett, Julius Caesar, Mark Antony

Women
1 Wonderwoman
2 Cleopatra
3 St Trinians
4 French maids
5 Elizabethan and Tudor
6 Showgirls and bunnygirls
7 Twenties' flappers
8 Indian squaws, cowgirls (especially Annie Oakley)
9 Saloon girls and French tarts
10 Georgian and Victorian

There is a growing trend, say Berman's, for people to want to look like Hollywood stars – the most popular being Marilyn Monroe and Errol Flynn (in Robin Hood garb). TV's Miss Piggy is another growing favourite. Berman's have over 4 000 different costumes of which up to 2 000 are hired out in any one week. Said a spokesman: 'One lady wanted to dress like a great bustard (bird) and a very conventional gentleman wished to wear a superman suit underneath his pinstripes so he could strip off during a very important business lunch.

'Generally speaking we get more men customers. Women are still a bit reluctant to live out their fantasies or make fools of themselves.'

FAVOURITES

Because we thought he'd know a bit about the subject, we asked Michael Parkinson to name his ten favourite ladies.

Michael Parkinson's ten favourite ladies

1 **Miss Piggy** – the sexiest bit of cloth I have ever seduced.
2 **Catherine Bramwell-Booth** – the great-granddaughter of the founder of the Salvation Army. She proves my theory that old people are the most interesting and the most honest to talk to.
3 **Dame Edith Evans** – for the same reasons.
4 **Diana Rigg** – she disproves the theory that all actresses are dim. She's bright, on any topic.
5 **Glenda Jackson** – another intelligent actress.
6 **Shirley McLaine** – it was one of my boyhood fantasies to run off with an American filmstar, a wise-cracking, leggy broad from New York. I still fancy her.
7 **Bette Midler** – another American star who is even more outrageous.
8 **Margot Fonteyn** – for a lady of middle years, she is astonishing. She's like a young girl.
9 **Erin Pizzey** – she's a very articulate lady, and I approve of what she stands for.
10 **The Wife – Mary Parkinson.** No, not because she'll read this but because I honestly think she's the best woman performer on TV. If she didn't have my name, she could be huge. She's a very good interviewer and she looks terrific.

Susan George's ten
favourite British actors

1 John Hurt
2 Richard Burton
3 Alan Bates
4 Edward Fox
5 Lord Olivier

6 Timothy West
7 Simon Ward
8 Peter O'Toole
9 Tom Courtenay
10 Paul Scofield

She comments: 'I think there's a wealth of acting talent in Britain which is why it is so difficult to compile a list of favourites. Tom Courtenay I've always admired enormously. I think he's underrated, but through choice. He's selective about his roles which makes him exclusive and elusive. I thought he was superb in *One Day In The Life Of Ivan Denisovich*.

'I became a fan of John Hurt after his TV role as Quentin Crisp in *The Naked Civil Servant* and his performances have gone from strength to strength. Paul Scofield I chose because of his mesmerizing performance in *A Man For All Seasons*; Richard Burton because I saw him on the stage in New York in *Equus* – in many ways a difficult play to understand – years ago. I was sitting in the front row and it was amazing how he simplified the story for me. I sent him a fan letter – my first – after the show, and then last year we worked together on a Bob Hope special and he thanked me for it.'

Joan Collins's ten most
charismatic British men

We asked her to name her sexiest men and she said certainly not . . .

1 **Paul McCartney** – has a little boy quality; is very together as a person and is one of the world's prolific songwriters.

2 **Mick Jagger** – raunchy, sexy, outrageous, eats up the stage as a performer: interesting off-stage.

3 **Albert Finney** – brilliant British stage actor: devastating, charming and fun in real life.

4 **Prince Andrew** – has the potential to outdo Prince Charles in the charm and daring stakes.

5 **Lord Goodman** – great presence and versatility, humorous, with an agile mind: he would have been a great politician.

6 **'Tiny' Rowland** – The word 'impossible' is not in his vocabulary.

7 **David Niven** – The most debonair and gentlemanly English actor. He has the quality of making you feel that when you're with him you are the only person in the world he wants to be with. Also a great raconteur.

8 **Sean Connery** – A truly masculine man, he gets better as he gets older. Does not mind about ageing or going bald and as a consequence is more attractive.

9 **Enoch Powell** – politically speaking not my cup of tea but he is an evocative, fascinating speaker.

10 **Kermit the Frog** – has mass appeal and is liked by children, women and men. Cheeky and outrageous, although not handsome.

FILMS

Top UK box office
receipts, 1979

Screen International

Moonraker is the fourth James Bond film to head the Top Twenty in the last ten years – *Diamonds are Forever* was top in 1972; *Live and Let Die* in 1973 and *The Spy Who Loved Me* in 1977.

film/distributor	*nationality*
1 *Moonraker* (UA)	Franco-British
Superman (Col–EMI–War)	British
2 *Jaws 2* (C/C)	American

3	*Every Which Way But Loose* (Col-EMI-War)	American
4	*Alien* (Twentieth-Century Fox)	British
5	*Watership Down* (C/C)	British
6	*The Deer Hunter* (Col-EMI-War)	American
7	*Grease* (C/C)	American
8	*Quadrophenia* (Brent Walker)	British
9	*Pete's Dragon* (Walt Disney)	American
10	*Midnight Express* (Col-EMI-War)	British
11	*National Lampoon's Animal House* (C/C)	American
12	*Death On The Nile* (Col-EMI-War)	British
13	*Porridge* (ITC)	British
14	*The Cat From Outer Space* (Walt Disney)	American
15	*Battlestar Galactica* (C/C)	American
16	*The Thirty-Nine Steps* (Rank)	British
	The Bitch (Brent Walker)	British
	Lord Of The Rings (UA)	American
17	*The Warriors* (C/C)	American
18	*Hooper* (Col-EMI-War)	American
19	*Piranha* (UA)	American
20	*Kentucky Fried Movie* (Alpha)	American
	Blazing Saddles/Monty Python and the Holy Grail (Col-EMI-War)	American/ British

FISH

Britain's fishing fleet

The total number of vessels at 31 December 1976 was 9 059. This consisted of 6 443 in England and Wales and 2 616 in Scotland.

Total landed weight (thousand tonnes)	917
Cod	211

Haddock	128
Herring	85
Shellfish	78
Saithe (coalfish)	40
Plaice	32
Other	343

Total value (£ thousand)	206 489
Cod	79 951
Haddock	34 858
Shellfish	21 539
Plaice	12 263
Herring	10 846
Saithe	6 970
Other	40 062

FIX ITS

Jimmy Savile's ten most enjoyable *Jim'll Fix It* programmes

Mr Savile receives approximately 30 000 *Fix It* letters a week. He says, 'For me it has become a way of life rather than a job and our team of workers is constantly fixing up something even if it doesn't appear on the show. Every *Jim'll Fix It*, big or small, is like a magic carpet, and very special to the kids involved.' Here are Jimmy's favourites:

1 A girl who wished to be filmed riding a white horse across the 'office atmosphere' of a news studio while a boy who wanted to be a newscaster read the news with Richard Baker: 'The only snag was the newsroom was on the sixth floor and we had to figure a way of getting the horse up there. We also had to lay some covering down in case the horse messed up the BBC floor.'

2 Mrs Howlett, a blind lady who sent in a piece of music she had herself composed which was subsequently arranged by Bob Sharples and conducted by Edward Heath.

3 Girl on a wing: An eighteen-year-old clerk wanted to stand on a wing of an aeroplane. She was assisted and trained by the Barnstormers Flying Circus: 'We had a radio mike attached to her and while she was in action we heard her say, "British Airways has nothing on this" . . .'

4 Wrestling with Big Daddy: a seven-year-old boy's ambition was to tag wrestle with the famous wrestler because 'Big Daddy never loses'.

5 Two girls who wanted to 'follow that cab' as in the movies were taken in a cab to Ardes in France in hot pursuit of another cab, which, when tracked down, was found to be carrying the mayor of Ardes. 'The funny thing was they'd missed the hovercraft to France so boarded the next one shouting, "follow that hovercraft". . .'

6 A boy who wanted to be a butler was taken to Ragley Hall in Warwickshire, which belongs to Lord Hertford, and trained with his butler, Mr Fobbester, whom he later assisted during a dinner party given by Lord Hertford.

7 Show jumping: a little girl who transformed her parents' back-garden into a mini-Hickstead with buckets, brooms and mops to construct a show-jumping course for pretend show jumping. Britain's top show jumpers Harvey Smith, David Broome and Caroline Bradley took part in the show. 'It was marvellous to see Harvey and the others jumping the course without a horse.' Raymond Brooks-Ward did the commentary.

8 A child wrote in requesting, 'Can I please polish a python,' so with the aid of some 'python polish', concocted by the Fix It team, a cloth and a duster, the child polished a python in the studios.

9 A girl who wanted a signed picture of Jimmy Savile was told she could take her own picture. She was taken to the RAF station in St Mawgan and flown in an RAF Nimrod over the Channel to take pictures of Jimmy Savile who was travelling on a ferry from Jersey. Jimmy signed her pictures in the studio.

10 Upstairs downstairs: octogenarian Mrs Goodenough

wanted to revisit Rhinefield House where she had worked as a chambermaid in her youth. As a surprise her friends and family were invited along to dinner at the house: 'It was just like *This Is Your Life.*' She said afterwards that if she died tomorrow it was the happiest day of her life. Sadly, she died three days later.

FLOWERS

The ten most popular
spring-flowering bulbs

1 Daffodil/narcissus
2 Tulip
3 Hyacinth
4 Crocus
5 Muscari – common name grape hyacinth
6 Scilla – common name squill
7 Galanthus – common name snowdrop
8 Iris (dwarf and Dutch iris)
9 Sparaxis – common name harlequin
10 Anemone

The ten most popular
summer-flowering bulbs

1 Dahlia
2 Gladiolus
3 Lily
4 Tuberous begonia
5 Anemone
6 Ranunculus
7 Montbretia

8 Ornithogalum thyrsoides – common name chicherinchee
9 Acidanthera
10 Tigridia – common name tiger flower

The majority of bulbs grown in Britain are imported from Holland. Britain has a large bulb industry but concentrates on the production of selected varieties of daffodils and tulips and these varieties are primarily used by the commercial grower to force into cut flowers and pot plants.

In 1978 the total volume of bulbs imported from Holland was 7 390 000 kilos, an increase in volume of 26% compared with 1977.

The most popular bulb grown *indoors* is, by far, the hyacinth.

FOOTBALL

Not content with dazzling us with his cricket knowledge, Nicholas Mason has also been through the records to create some football lists.

The hat-trick men

Sixty-one hat-tricks (three goals by an individual in one match) have been scored by England footballers in internationals since 1872; thirty-two have been scored by Scotland footballers; ten for Wales and six for Northern Ireland (known as Ireland up to 1946).

Twelve men have scored more than one hat-trick for one or other of the Home countries in international football. They are:

Six times :   JIMMY GREAVES (England) (1960 – 66)
Four times :   V. J. WOODWARD (England) (1908–9)
              BOBBY CHARLTON (England) (1959–63)

Three times :	R. S. McCOLL (Scotland) (1899–1900)
	HUGHIE GALLACHER (Scotland) (1926–9)
	STANLEY MORTENSEN (England) (1947–8)
	DENIS LAW (Scotland) (1962–3)
Twice :	STEVE BLOOMER (England) (1896–1901)
	R. C. HAMILTON (Scotland) (1901–2)
	'DIXIE' DEAN (England) (1927)
	GEORGE CAMSELL (England) (1929)
	TOMMY LAWTON (England) (1946–7)

The hat-trick plus men

On thirty-six occasions, a player has scored four goals or more in a match for one of the Home countries. They are:

For England (21)
O. H. VAUGHTON (5 goals) v Ireland, 1882
A. BROWN (4) v Ireland, 1882
B. W. SPILSBURY (4) v Ireland, 1886
S. BLOOMER (5) v Wales, 1896
G. O. SMITH (4) v Ireland, 1899
S. BLOOMER (4) v Wales, 1901
V. J. WOODWARD (4) v Austria, 1908
G. R. HILSDON (4) v Hungary, 1908
V. J. WOODWARD (4) v Hungary, 1909
G. H. CAMSELL (4) v Belgium, 1929
G. W. HALL (5) v Ireland, 1938
T. LAWTON (4) v Netherlands, 1946
T. LAWTON (4) v Portugal, 1947
S. MORTENSEN (4) v Portugal, 1947
J. F. ROWLEY (4) v N. Ireland, 1949
T. FINNEY (4) v Portugal, 1950
D. J. WILSHAW (4) v Scotland, 1955
J. GREAVES (4) v N. Ireland, 1963
R. HUNT (4) v USA, 1964
J. GREAVES (4) v Norway, 1966
M. MACDONALD (5) v Cyprus, 1975

For Scotland (12)
A. HIGGINS (4) v Ireland, 1885
C. HEGGIE (5) v Ireland, 1886
W. PAUL (4) v Wales, 1890
J. MADDEN (4) v Wales, 1893
A. MCMAHON (4) v Ireland, 1901
R. C. HAMILTON (4) v Ireland, 1901
J. QUINN (4) v Ireland, 1908
H. K. GALLACHER (4) v Wales, 1928
W. STEEL (4) v N. Ireland, 1950
D. LAW (4) v N. Ireland, 1962
D. LAW (4) v Norway, 1963
C. STEIN (4) v Cyprus, 1969

For Wales (3)
J. PRICE (4) v Ireland, 1882
J. DOUGHTY (4) v Ireland, 1888
M. CHARLES (4) v N. Ireland, 1962

No Northern Ireland player has scored more than three goals in an international match.

These we have cheered

A list of the Football League clubs that have disappeared from the League since the War.

Accrington Stanley	(original members of the League. In League 1888–93 and 1921–62.) *Replaced by Oxford United*
Barrow	(In League 1921–72; not re-elected) *Replaced by Hereford United*
Bradford Park Avenue	(In League 1908–70; not re-elected) *Replaced by Cambridge United*
Gateshead	(In League 1919–30 as South Shields, and 1930–60 as Gateshead; not re-elected) *Replaced by Peterborough United*

New Brighton	(In League 1898–1902, and 1923–51; not re-elected)
	Replaced by Workington
Southport	(In League 1921–78; not re-elected)
	Replaced by Wigan Athletic
Workington	(In League 1951–77; not re-elected)
	Replaced by Wimbledon

Cup specialists

Up to 1980, thirty clubs, some of them now extinct, had reached the FA Cup Final on three occasions or more:

11	Newcastle United (6 wins)
	Arsenal (5 wins)
10	West Bromwich Albion (5 wins)
9	Aston Villa (7 wins)
8	Blackburn Rovers (6 wins)
	Manchester United (4 wins)
	Wolverhampton Wanderers (4 wins)
7	Bolton Wanderers (4 wins)
	Preston North End (2 wins)
	Everton (3 wins)
	Manchester City (4 wins)
6	Liverpool (2 wins)
	Old Etonians (2 wins)
	Sheffield United (4 wins)
5	Huddersfield Town (1 win)
	The Wanderers (5 wins)
	Sheffield Wednesday (3 wins)
	Tottenham Hotspur (5 wins)
4	West Ham United (3 wins)
	Derby County (1 win)
	Oxford University (1 win)
	Royal Engineers (1 win)
	Leeds United (1 win)
	Leicester City (no wins)
3	Blackpool (1 win)

Burnley (1 win)
Chelsea (1 win)
Portsmouth (1 win)
Sunderland (2 wins)
Southampton (1 win)

Worst cup sides

Football League teams which have recorded least progress over the history of the FA Cup.

Never beyond the Fourth Round
Cambridge United
Hartlepool United
Hereford United
Rochdale
Torquay United
Wigan Athletic
Wimbledon

Never beyond the Fifth Round
Aldershot
Brighton & Hove Albion
Chester
Chesterfield
Darlington
Doncaster Rovers
Gillingham
Halifax Town
Lincoln City
Newport County
Northampton Town
Plymouth Argyle
Rotherham United
Scunthorpe United
Southend United
Stockport County
Tranmere Rovers
Walsall

Football crowds, 1978-9

Jake Davies, our resident calculator, has been taking a look at attendance figures during the 1978–9 season.

The ten highest Football League average attendances (home and away)

			league position	
1	Liverpool	41 677	1	
2	Manchester United	38 402	9	
3	Spurs	33 955	11	
4	Everton	33 173	4	
5	Arsenal	32 375	7	All
6	Manchester City	32 187	15	teams
7	Notts Forest	30 825	2	First
8	Aston Villa	30 141	8	Division
9	Leeds United	29 096	5	
10	West Bromwich Albion	27 366	3	

The ten lowest Football League average attendances (home and away)

			league position	
1	Halifax Town	2 772	23	
2	Rochdale	2 780	20	
3	Crewe Alexandra	2 784	24	
4	Darlington	2 954	21	
5	Torquay United	3 252	11	All
6	Northampton Town	3 273	19	teams
7	Scunthorpe United	3 353	12	Fourth
8	Doncaster Rovers	3 418	22	Division
9	York City	3 437	10	
10	Hartlepool United	3 524	13	

Footballers of the year

Elected annually since 1947–8 by the Football Writers' Association.

1947–8	Stanley Matthews
1948–9	Johnny Carey
1949–50	Joe Mercer
1950–51	Harry Johnston
1951–2	Billy Wright
1952–3	Nat Lofthouse
1953–4	Tom Finney
1954–5	Don Revie
1955–6	Bert Trautmann
1956–7	Tom Finney
1957–8	Danny Blanchflower
1958–9	Sid Owens
1959–60	Bill Slater
1960–61	Danny Blanchflower
1961–2	Jimmy Adamson
1962–3	Stanley Matthews
1963–4	Bobby Moore
1964–5	Bobby Collins
1965–6	Bobby Charlton
1966–7	Jackie Charlton
1967–8	George Best
1968–9	Dave Mackay and Tony Book
1969–70	Billy Bremner
1970–71	Frank McLintock
1971–2	Gordon Banks
1972–3	Pat Jennings
1973–4	Ian Callaghan
1974–5	Alan Mullery
1975–6	Kevin Keegan
1976–7	Emlyn Hughes
1977–8	Kenny Burns
1978–9	Kenny Dalglish
1979–80	Terry McDermott

Longest-serving footballers

These are the players in the history of English Football League who have played the most competitive games for the same club.

	games
Jimmy Dickinson, Portsmouth	764
Roy Sproson, Port Vale	761
John Trollope, Swindon	756
Terry Paine, Southampton	713
Ron Harris, Chelsea	641
Ian Callaghan, Liverpool	640
Jack Charlton, Leeds	629
Joe Shaw, Sheffield United	629

The list was correct up to January 1980, by which time only Ron Harris, Chelsea, was still playing for the same club. Ian Callaghan, though still playing football, had moved to Swansea.

Jasper Carrott's favourite footballers

Mr Carrott is a Director of Birmingham City FC and a regular full-back for his local team, Hockley Heath Rangers. 'Not the obscure Hockley Heath Rangers. THE Hockley Heath Rangers.' These are his favourite footballers, with comments. The best player he's ever seen is Johann Cruyff of Holland but in this book we are only concerned with British people.

1 **Malcolm MacDonald**, ex-Newcastle United and Arsenal. 'I like him as a player and as a person.'

2 **Trevor Francis**, Nottingham Forest. 'Britain's most skilful player.'

3 **Gary Pendrey**, West Bromwich Albion. 'He's your bog standard ace, a Club prop. Without him, football would not exist.'

76

4 **Stanley Matthews,** ex-Blackpool. 'I've had my photograph taken with him, haven't I? That was a great ambition achieved.'
5 **Joe Mercer,** ex-Arsenal. 'He's the England team's most successful manager. He didn't lose a match – and he's one of the nicest people I've met.'
6 **Eddie Brown,** ex-Birmingham City. 'I used to watch him as a boy. He was a real clown. He used to shake hands with policemen and corner flags.'
7 **Jimmy Greaves,** ex-Tottenham Hotspur. 'Apart from his obvious goal-scoring feats, I think the way he's come through his tragedy since then (his alcoholism) with such dignity is an example to us all.'

FRAGRANCE

The ten most popular perfumes
Audits of Great Britain

The total perfume market for 1979 was worth £91 million. The brand share for that year is as follows:

 1 'Charlie' by Revlon – 7%
 2 'Youth Dew' by Estée Lauder – 6%
 3 'No 5' by Chanel – 3%
 4 'Tweed' by Lenthéric – 2%
 5 'Panache' by Lenthéric – 2%
 6 'Blasé' by Max Factor – 2%
 7 'L'Aimant' by Coty – 2%
 8 'Tramp' by Lenthéric – 2 %
 9 'Intimate' by Revlon – 2%
10 'Cachet' by Prince Matchebelli – 1%

According to Revlon, what women look for in perfumes are tenacity, and a smell that they can relate to. 'But it is also a question of what suits you too. What may smell nice on one woman might not smell as nice on another.'

Perfume is inextricably bound-up with image. 'Charlie', the UK and world market leader, is successful because it conjures up images of fresh, young and lively women. 'It has a well-balanced bouquet with both floral and citrus scents, and it is very modern and still feminine.'

GALLERIES AND MUSEUMS

Attendances at major art galleries and museums

Art Galleries	1966	1971	1976	1977	1978
			thousands		
National Gallery	1521	1859	2354	2686	2501
Tate Gallery	894	936	1202	1006	1081
Royal Academy	300	250	389	1150	850
National Portrait Gallery	248	513	324	535	425
Hayward Gallery		137	414	92	342
Scottish National Gallery	207	241	175	171	235
Serpentine Gallery		55	132	173	229
Museums					
British Museum	1808	2680	3964	4124	4034
Science Museum	1700	1942	2508	3361	3486
Natural History Museum	1059	1576	2703	3193	2788
Victoria and Albert Museum	1322	2034	1552	2340	1934
National Railway Museum, York			1830	1440	1486
Imperial War Museum	431	557	726	1090	1435
National Maritime Museum	786	1591	1700	1250	1260
Royal Scottish Museum	533	534	608	611	646
Geological Museum	367	345	496	510	531
National Museum of Wales	372	383	287	337	328
Welsh Folk Museum	123	185	285	269	288

GARDENS

Best British gardens

Ten of the best British gardens, all in private ownership and all open to the public, compiled specially by the Historic Houses Association Gardens Committee.

1 **Tresco Abbey**, Isles of Scilly – the only important collection of sub-tropical plants in the British Isles.
2 **Leonardslee**, Horsham, Sussex – the greatest creation of the Loder family of gardeners. Outstanding rhododendron collection.
3 **Borde Hill**, Sussex – an important collection of trees and shrubs, including late Victorian plants.
4 **Castle Howard**, Yorkshire – a garden containing many outstanding features, including some recently established shrub roses.
5 **Arley Hall Garden**, Cheshire – an old-fashioned English garden in the heart of Cheshire.
6 **Pusey House**, Faringdon, Oxon – a modern garden with excellent herbaceous borders and sweeping lawns.
7 **Great Dixter**, Northiam, Sussex – a supreme 'plantsman's' garden much influenced by the great gardener, Gertrude Jekyll.
8 **Hergest Croft**, Kington, Herefordshire – contains an important collection of trees and shrubs.
9 **Crarae Lodge**, Argyll – trees and shrubs of great distinction.
10 **Kiftsgate Court**, Gloucestershire – a romantic Cotswold garden with shrubs rambling over a steep escarpment.

GOLF

Oldest golf clubs

Britain's oldest golf clubs, with the dates of their foundation. Almost all are Scottish.

1735	Royal Burgess Golfing Society, Edinburgh
1744	Honourable Company of Edinburgh Golfers
1754	Royal and Ancient, St Andrews
1761	Bruntsfield Links, Edinburgh
1774	Royal Musselburgh
1780	Royal Aberdeen
1786	Crail Golfing Society
1787	Royal Blackheath (traditionally founded in 1605 though this is not provable)
1787	Glasgow
1794	Dunbar
1797	Burntisland
1810	Royal Albert, Montrose
1817	Scotscraig, Tayport
1818	Royal Manchester
1820	Inverleven
1824	Royal Perth Golfing Society
1829	Royal Calcutta
1832	North Berwick
1839	Carnoustie
1840	Leven

Best British performance in
each British Open Championship
for the last twenty years

Tony Jacklin, in 1969, has so far been the only British winner
of our own competition.

year	course	player	position	score
1960	St Andrews	Bernard Hunt	= 3rd	282
1961	Birkdale	Dai Rees	2nd	285
1962	Troon	Brian Huggett	= 3rd	289
1963	Lytham	A. G. King	= 11th	289
		Bernard Hunt	= 11th	289
1964	St Andrews	Bernard Hunt	4th	287
1965	Birkdale	Brian Huggett	= 2nd	287
1966	Muirfield	Dave Thomas	= 2nd	283
1967	Hoylake	Clive Clark	= 3rd	284
1968	Carnoustie	Maurice Bembridge	5th	293
1969	Lytham	Tony Jacklin	1st	280
1970	St Andrews	Tony Jacklin	5th	286
1971	Birkdale	Tony Jacklin	3rd	280
1972	Muirfield	Tony Jacklin	3rd	280
1973	Troon	Neil Coles	= 2nd	279
1974	Lytham	Peter Oosterhuis	2nd	286
1975	Carnoustie	Peter Oosterhuis	= 7th	282
		Neil Coles	= 7th	282
1976	Birkdale	Mark James	= 5th	288
1977	Turnberry	Tommy Horton	= 9th	284
1978	St Andrews	Peter Oosterhuis	6th	284
1979	Lytham	Mark James	4th	287

Dickie Henderson's best
British golf courses

We could have got a professional golfer to tell us his favourites,
or a park keeper, but we decided to ask a professional

entertainer, who maintains he has a handicap of 8, to give us the benefit of the many hours he's wasted on British greens. Ladies and gentlemen, Dickie Henderson ...

1 **Royal Berkshire** – it suits my slice because I can play three courses, the Berkshire, Wentworth and Sunningdale, all on the same day and during the same round.

2 **Gleneagles** – a marvellous, testing course, known throughout the world.

3 **Woodhall Spa**, Lincolnshire

4 **Sunningdale** – Berkshire

5 **Troon** – Ayrshire. The course on which Gene Sarazan holed in one at the famous Postage Stamp hole in the first round of the Open a few years back. In the second round, he did it in two. I remember it because when I played that hole I made a seven and an eight!

6 **Rosemount** Stirlingshire – another very good Scottish course.

7 **Muirfield**, Scotland

8 **Port Marnock**, Eire

9 **Princess**, Sandwich, Kent

10 **St Andrews** – I kept that for last. A course to grace any list of top golf courses, not only in Britain, but in the whole world.

GOSSIP

Most-gossiped-about people

Nigel Dempster's fifteen most-gossiped about celebrities, in order of the frequency of mentions in British gossip columns, 1979.

1 Jacqueline Onassis
2 Prince Charles
3 Bianca Jagger
4 Princess Caroline of Monaco
5 Christina Onassis
6 The Shah of Iran
7 Princess Margaret and Roddy Llewellyn
8 Edward Kennedy

9 Britt Ekland
10 Soraya Khashoggi
11 Margaret Trudeau
12 Regine

13 Elizabeth Taylor
14 Warren Beatty
15 Prince Andrew

'Jackie Onassis is still the favourite,' says Nigel Dempster, 'because she married a President of the United States and then a rich old frog years older than her.

'Obviously the celebrities themselves have to keep in the limelight in order to get in the papers. If they go off the boil, that's it. Showbiz people are very popular as they are more readily identifiable than, say, the aristocracy, who don't appear on TV every week. Royalty, however, is a hardy perennial, year in, year out. People see them as untouchables so they like it when they're seen as human beings: breaking their legs, losing their dogs or breaking up their marriages.'

GRAFFITI

Some of Britain's graffiti has been on the same walls for as long as fifty years and shows no sign of disappearing, although local authorities now organize graffiti-removing squads armed with chemical solvents. Graffiti has been with us a long time: in the eighteenth century, self-appointed guardians of morals used to carry around a damp sponge to wipe away obscene and blasphemous scrawls.

Incidentally, according to Nigel Rees, the best place in the UK to go in search of interesting graffiti, apart from the university towns, is Brighton.

Twenty examples of
graffiti in the Seventies

Graffiti Lives OK by Nigel Rees (Unwin Paperbacks)

1 Prepare to meet thy God (evening dress optional).
2 Women like the simpler things in life – like men.
3 Drink wet cement and get really stoned.
4 The grave of Karl Marx is just another communist plot.
5 God is not dead, but alive and well and working on a much less ambitious project.
6 Death is nature's way of telling you to slow down.
7 Conserve energy – make love more slowly.
8 Nostalgia is all right, but not what it used to be.
9 Keep Britain tidy – kill a tourist.
10 Not for sale during the French postal strike (written on a contraceptive-vending machine).
11 Before you meet your handsome prince you have to kiss a lot of toads.
12 Tolkien is hobbit-forming.
13 When God made man she was only testing.
14 Racial prejudice is a pigment of the imagination.
15 Rugby is a game played by gentlemen with odd-shaped balls.
16 Reality is for people who can't cope with their drugs.
17 You're never alone with schizophrenia.
18 TV sets guaranteed working perfect – as advertised on Police 5.
19 Humpty Dumpty was pushed.
20 A happy Christmas to all our readers.

GRAND PRIX

First run as the RAC Grand Prix at Brooklands in 1926, the name British Grand Prix was first used in 1949. This is a full list of winners, circuits and distance. No sign of Mark Thatcher so far...

	driver	car	circuit	distance (miles)	speed (mph)
1926	Robert Senechal/Louis Wagner	Delage	Brooklands	287	71·61
1927	Robert Benoist	Delage	Brooklands	325	85·59
*1935	Richard Shuttleworth	Alfa Romeo	Donington	306	63·97
1936	Hans Ruesch/Richard Seaman	Alfa Romeo	Donington	306	69·23
1937	Bernd Rosemeyer	Auto-Union	Donington	250	82·85
1938	Tazio Nuvolari	Auto-Union	Donington	250	80·49
1948	Luigi Villoresi	Maserati	Silverstone	250	72·28
1949	Baron Emmanuel de Graffenried	Maserati	Silverstone	300	77·31
1950	Giuseppe Farina	Alfa Romeo	Silverstone	202	90·95
1951	Froilan Gonzalez	Ferrari	Silverstone	253	96·11
1952	Alberto Ascari	Ferrari	Silverstone	249	90·92
1953	Alberto Ascari	Ferrari	Silverstone	263	92·97
1954	Froilan Gonzalez	Ferrari	Silverstone	270	89·69
*1955	Stirling Moss	Mercedes-Benz	Aintree	270	86·47
1956	Juan Manuel Fangio	Ferrari	Silverstone	300	98·65
*1957	Tony Brooks/Stirling Moss	Vanwall	Aintree	270	86·80

*British winners

Continued on next page

	driver	car	circuit	distance (miles)	speed (mph)
*1958	Peter Collins	Ferrari	Silverstone	225	102·05
1959	Jack Brabham	Cooper–Climax	Aintree	225	89·88
1960	Jack Brabham	Cooper–Climax	Silverstone	231	108·69
1961	Wolfgang von Trips	Ferrari	Aintree	225	83·91
*1962	Jim Clark	Lotus–Climax	Aintree	225	92·25
*1963	Jim Clark	Lotus–Climax	Silverstone	246	107·75
*1964	Jim Clark	Lotus–Climax	Brands Hatch	212	94·14
*1965	Jim Clark	Lotus–Climax	Silverstone	240	112·02
1966	Jack Brabham	Repco Brabham	Brands Hatch	212	95·48
*1967	Jim Clark	Lotus–Ford	Silverstone	240	117·64
1968	Joseph Siffert	Lotus–Ford	Brands Hatch	212	104·83
*1969	Jackie Stewart	Matra–Ford	Silverstone	246	127·25
1970	Jochen Rindt	Lotus–Ford	Brands Hatch	212	108·69
*1971	Jackie Stewart	Tyrrell–Ford	Silverstone	199	130·48
1972	Emerson Fittipaldi	JPS–Ford	Brands Hatch	201	112·06
1973	Peter Revson	McLaren–Ford	Silverstone	196	131·75
1974	Jody Scheckter	Tyrrell–Ford	Brands Hatch	199	115·73
1975	Emerson Fittipaldi	McLaren–Ford	Silverstone	164	120·01
1976	Niki Lauda	Ferrari	Brands Hatch	198	114·24
*1977	James Hunt	McLaren–Ford	Silverstone	199	130·36
1978	Carlos Reutemann	Ferrari	Brands Hatch	199	116·61
1979	'Clay' Regazzoni	Saudia–Williams	Silverstone	199	138·80

*British winners

British world champions

The world drivers' championship has been won by a British driver on ten occasions since the championship was instituted in 1950.

1958	Mike Hawthorn
1962	Graham Hill
1963	Jim Clark
1964	John Surtees
1965	Jim Clark
1968	Graham Hill
1969	Jackie Stewart
1971	Jackie Stewart
1973	Jackie Stewart
1976	James Hunt

GROCERS

AGB Research

Britain's top grocers, according to their share of the total grocery market, 1980.

Co-op grocers	17·4%
Tesco	13·6%
Sainsbury	11·9%
Asda	7·3%
Independent grocers	7·2%
International Stores	5·2%
Fine Fare	5·0%
Kwiksave	4·9%
Allied Suppliers	4·8%
Spar	3·2%
Marks & Spencer	1·9%
Keymarket	1·8%

VG	1·6%
Mace	1·5%
Waitrose	1·3%
Safeway	1·2%
Boots	0·8%
Woolworth	0·7%

The remainder of the market is divided among the thousands of little shops that line our high streets.

HEAVIEST MPs

The General Election in May 1979 brought in a good new batch of fatties, to join the existing heavyweights, but no one quite reached Cyril Smith's proportions and he remains the outright winner in this brand-new contest. The weights are all estimates, but based on first-hand observation by a well known parliamentary expert, who wishes to remain anonymous, just in case anyone sits on him. (Any MP who feels he has been misused should furnish proof of his correct weight.)

Cyril Smith	27	stones
Iain Mills	20	"
Donald Thompson	18	"
Peter Emery	18	"
Rev. Ian Paisley	18	"
Martin Stevens	18	"
Geraint Morgan	17	"
Eric Heffer	17	"
Russell Kerr	17	"
Harry Cowans	17	"
Edward Heath	17	"
Geoffrey Dickens	16	"
Graham Bright	16	"
Hector Monroe	16	"
Michael Jopling	16	"

Robert Taylor   16   "
Spencer le Marchant   16   "
John Stokes   16   "

HEROES AND HEROINES

During 1979 Madame Tussaud's handed out over 500 000 of their annual questionnaires to visitors in their London exhibition to discover people's heroes and heroines. The visitors could choose anyone in the whole world, not necessarily someone whose effigy appears in Tussaud's, though one question was included which was purely on their exhibits. There was also one question on the most hated and feared people.

British people's
favourite people

(According to a poll conducted amongst visitors to Tussaud's, London, 1979)

POLITICS (1978 placings in brackets)
1 Mrs Thatcher (Jimmy Carter)
2 Jimmy Carter (Mrs Thatcher)
3 David Steel (President Sadat)
4 Cyril Smith (Winston Churchill)
5 J. F. Kennedy (Edward Heath)

SPORT
1 Bjorn Borg (Muhammad Ali)
2 Muhammad Ali (Pele)
3 Kevin Keegan (Kevin Keegan)
4 Pele (Bjorn Borg)
5 Sebastian Coe (Ilie Nastase)

ENTERTAINMENT
1 Freddie Starr (Bruce Forsyth)
2 Ronnie Barker (Elton John)
3 Telly Savalas (Charlie Chaplin)
4 Frank Sinatra (Liza Minnelli)
5 Elvis Presley (Frank Sinatra)

ARTS
1 Picasso (Picasso)
2 Margot Fonteyn (Margot Fonteyn)
3 Dali (Dali)
4 Constable (Rembrandt)
5 van Gogh (Rudolf Nureyev)

BEAUTY
1 Sophia Loren (Sophia Loren)
2 Debbie Harry (Marilyn Monroe)
3 Brigitte Bardot (Elizabeth Taylor)
4 Marilyn Monroe (Liza Minnelli)
5 Raquel Welch (Raquel Welch)

HERO OR HEROINE OF ALL TIME
1 Winston Churchill (Winston Churchill)
2 Joan of Arc (Superman)
3 Mountbatten (Muhammad Ali)
4 Lord Nelson (Lord Nelson)
5 Bjorn Borg (J. F. Kennedy)

FAVOURITE HERO OR HEROINE IN MADAME TUSSAUD'S
1 Kojak – Telly Savalas (Agatha Christie)
2 Elvis Presley (Kojak – Telly Savalas)
3 Bjorn Borg (Elton John)
4 Pope John Paul II (Elvis Presley)
5 The Queen (The Queen)

Person most hated and feared

1 Ayatollah Khomeini (Adolf Hitler)
2 Idi Amin (Idi Amin)
3 Adolf Hitler (Mrs Thatcher)
4 Dracula (Dracula)
5 The Yorkshire Ripper (Jack the Ripper)

In the Hate list, Hitler has dropped from number one to number three. Mrs Thatcher dropped completely from the Hate list – having emerged on the Political list as the number one favourite. Sic transit.

HISTORIC SIGHTS

Historic buildings attracting more than 200 000 paid admissions in 1978

English Tourist Board

NB Historic buildings to which entry is free, such as Westminster Abbey, are not included in this list.

Tower of London	3 005 000
State apartments, Windsor Castle	940 000
Stonehenge, Wiltshire	795 000
Roman Baths and Pump Room, Bath, Avon	794 000
St George's Chapel, Windsor, Berkshire	700 000
Hampton Court, London	660 000
Beaulieu, Hampshire	649 000
Shakespeare's birthplace, Warwickshire	640 000
Warwick Castle, Warwickshire	517 000
Anne Hathaway's Cottage, Warwickshire	479 000
Royal Pavilion, Brighton, East Sussex	409 000

Salisbury Cathedral, Wiltshire	378 000
Osborne House, Isle of Wight	292 000
Harewood House, West Yorkshire	273 000
Fountains Abbey, North Yorkshire	240 000
Dodington House, Avon	228 000
Brontë Parsonage, Haworth, West Yorkshire	214 000
Dover Castle, Kent	214 000
Assembly Rooms, Bath, Avon	207 000

Blenheim Palace, Chatsworth, Longleat and Woburn Abbey – all privately owned homes – do not reveal admissions, but they each had over 200 000 visitors in 1978.

HOLIDAYS

Holiday visitors to Britain

British Tourist Authority

In 1978, Britain earned more than £3 000 m in foreign exchange, the highest total ever. Over 12 500 000 visitors arrived during the year.

Foreign visitors, 1978

1	USA	1 964 000
2	W. Germany	1 507 000
3	France	1 435 000
4	Netherlands	1 003 000
5	Scandinavia	937 000
6	Irish Republic	873 000
7	Belgium/Luxembourg	740 000
8	Middle East	638 000
9	Canada	511 000
10	Australia/New Zealand	442 000

Expenditure by foreign holiday makers, 1978

		£ million
1	Shopping	832
2	Accommodation	800
3	Fares paid to British air and shipping lines on travel to and from Britain	687
4	Eating and drinking out	460
5	Internal transport	250
6	Entertainment, recreation	160
	Total	3 189

Despite inflation, most of the money was spent shopping – £250 m of it going on footwear and textiles.

London was as usual the most popular destination for overseas visitors (46%). Scotland was also very popular – 11% spending some part of their holidays there.

About 1½ m people throughout the whole of Britain depend, directly or indirectly, on tourism for their living.

Holidays taken by British people

The total number of holidays at home or abroad taken by residents of Great Britain was 48 million in 1978, higher than in 1976 and 1977, but not as high as the 1973 peak. Around 39 million holidays were taken in Britain. The number of holidays taken abroad increased to a record 9 million. Spain remained the most popular foreign destination (30% of all foreign holidays were taken there), followed by France, Italy and Greece. However, 39% of adults took no holiday (either at home or abroad) in 1978.

NOTE: a holiday is defined as at least four days away from home for non-business purposes.

Holidays abroad: destination (adults only)	Percentage of Britons visiting
Spain	30
France	14
Italy	8
Greece	7
Irish Republic	5
W. Germany	4
Belgium and Luxembourg	2
Netherlands	2
Austria	2
Switzerland	2
Eastern Europe	1

Thomas Cook's most expensive holidays, 1980

1 Far Eastern fly/cruise – 19 days, full board, £1 820
2 Barbados – 21 days, half board, £1 800
3 China air/rail/coach – 23 days, full board, £1 796
4 South America tour air/coach/rail – 22 days, full board £1 350
5 St Lucia – 21 days, half board, £999.
6 Himalayan Journey – 20 days, full board, £983.
7 Grand Coach Tour of Europe – 25 days, full board, £810.
8 Marbella, Spain – 2 weeks, half board, £738.
9 Las Palmas, Spain – 2 weeks, half board, £654.
10 Madeira (Reid's Hotel) – 14 days, bed and breakfast, £543.

Thomas Cook has always been a pioneer of travel, ever since he planned his first trip in 1841, from Leicester to Loughborough. Today, the firm which bears his name has a 40-strong reservation list of passengers for the first commercial flight to the moon.

In case China appeals to you for your next holiday, here are a few tips:

Eleven things to
take to China

Virginia Kelly, The Travel Agent, *December, 1979.*

1 Facial tissues
2 Soap flakes or powdered soap
3 Pre-moistened paper hand towels
4 Eye wash (air pollution is monumental)
5 Glue (stamps are ungummed)
6 Beer can opener (for fruit juice in hotel room)
7 Diarrhoea medicine
8 Rubber-soled shoes (the Great Wall is slippery)
9 Mosquito repellent
10 Light plastic mac
11 Plastic flask for drinking water

HORSE RACING

The fastest post-war
Derby winners

1 NIJINSKY (Lester Piggott, 1970) 2 min 34·68 sec
2 HENBIT (Willie Carson, 1980) 2 min 34·77 sec
3 SNOW KNIGHT (Brian Taylor, 1974) 2 min 35·04 sec
4 SHIRLEY HEIGHTS (Greville Starkey, 1978) 2 min 35·30 sec
5 GRUNDY (Pat Eddery, 1975) 2 min 35·35 sec
6 CREPELLO (Lester Piggott, 1957) 2 min 35·40 sec
7 PINZA (Gordon Richards, 1953) 2 min 35·60 sec
8 EMPERY (Lester Piggott, 1976) 2 min 35·69 sec
9 NEVER SAY DIE (Lester Piggott, 1954) 2 min 35·80 sec
  ST PADDY (Lester Piggott, 1960) 2 min 35·80 sec
11 MORSTON (Edward Hide, 1973) 2 min 35·92 sec
12 PARTHIA (Harry Carr, 1959) 2 min 36·00 sec

HOUSE NAMES

In order of popularity, these are the top ten types of names which people have chosen for their private houses. It is based on the recent survey which lecturer Joyce Miles has made of the house names in twenty towns and villages in England and Wales.

1 *Transferred place-names*
a Home towns – Londoners retiring to Cornwall and calling their new home Ilford, or northerners moving south but taking Oldham with them.
b Honeymoons and holidays – in the Thirties they went to Windermere and Braemar, then remembered it forever in their suburban semi. Today, the package boom brings back Tossa, Rimini, Marbella and San Remo – a list still growing.

2 *Trees*
For 150 years, The Elms has been most popular – including variations like Elmsleigh and Elmdene – but will it survive Dutch elm disease? After The Elms come Hollies, Beeches, Silver Birch, Twin Oaks.

3 *Flowers*
The rose is definitely first, in all its variations – Rose Cottage, Rosedene, Rosedale, Rosebank.

4 *Animals*
Fox Dell, Squirrels' Wood, Badgers' Croft. The Rookery is less popular today, as are all house names based on birds.

5 *Colours*
Green wins, usually combined with another element – Green Bank, Green Pastures. Second is grey with Greystones most popular.

6 *Location*
Depending on where the house is, or where the owner likes to believe it is – Fair View, Hill Top, Cornerways.

7 *Christian names*
Popular for over 100 years – think of Algernon Lodge and Eustace Villa, Gertiville and Normanhurst. The new fashion is for compound names – Chrisden, Davisal, Cinjon, Brydor.

8 *Foreign phrases*
Chez Nous of course, plus Shangri-la and Mon Repos, all old favourites. Coming up – Bella Vista and Casa Mia.

9 *Literary*
Jalna (from the novels of Mazo de la Roche); names from Tolkien have arrived in the last five years, such as Rivendell and The Hobbitt.

10 *Humorous*
Dunromin, Stoneybroke, Costalot have always been popular, but a new saucier strain has appeared – Knickers and Cobblers both increasing.

Witty names generally are the fastest growing category, but not expected to rival transferred place names, still the biggest section and thought to be good for another 100 years.

HOUSEPLANTS

Every year, over 250 million houseplants are sold in Britain. These are the most popular, according to a list compiled by Rochford's, a major plant nursery.

1 African violet
2 Poinsettia
3 Chrysanthemum
4 Cyclamen
5 Ficus robusta (Rubber plant)
6 Monstera (Swiss Cheese plant)
7 Ivy

8 Begonia, 'Fireglow'
9 Hibiscus
10 Chlorophytum

Britain is fast becoming a nation of indoor plant growers, as increasing sales figures show. Jock Davidson of Rochford's says: 'We sell approximately four million houseplants a year, and the figures are rising every year.

'Internationally, Britain is still pretty low in the world league, compared with Germany, Denmark and Holland. We haven't reached the Dutch "tiered ledges" stage yet. But there are very few homes in Britain today without any plants.'

HUSBANDS

Commission of the European Communities (From the Book of Numbers, *Heron House, 1979)*

Women in several European countries were asked if their husbands ever helped with housework. This is the percentage of women in each country who replied 'frequently':

Helpful husbands

Denmark	28·1
UK	22·7
Netherlands	21·2
France	19·6
W. Germany	14·8
Ireland	14·0
Italy	8·1

INTELLIGENCE

There is no foolproof way of measuring intelligence, not even IQ tests, but graduating from a university must prove something. Here are the areas of England inhabited by arguably the most intelligent people. It is based on local education authority reports published by the Department of Education.

Highest percentage of the population with university degrees, 1978

1	Richmond upon Thames	16·5
2	Surrey (as a whole)	14·8
3	Bromley	13·4
4	Barnet	13·3
5	Stockport	12·7
6	Buckinghamshire	12·4
7	Kingston upon Thames	12·4
8	Harrow	12·0
9	Sutton	11·6
10	Oxfordshire	11·5

Lowest percentage of the population with university degrees, 1978

1	Barking	2·0
2	Newham	2·5
3	Sandwell	3·0
4	Knowsley	3·5
5	Thameside	4·8
6	Oldham	5·3
7	Manchester	5·6
8	Walsall	5·8
9	Gateshead	5·8
10	Wigan	5·9

JOKERS

Jasper Carrott's
funniest people

1 John Cleese
2 Blaster Bates
3 Eric Idle
4 Spike Milligan
5 Jake Thackray
6 Jeremy Taylor
7 Billy Connolly
8 Mike Harding
9 The cast of *Crossroads*

These are Mr Carrott's personal favourites in Britain. In his all-star list to joke with the Mars first eleven he would also consider the Americans Bob Newhart, Tom Lehrer, Bill Cosby, Steve Martin and George Carlin.

And now for something which could have been very similar, though only Spike Milligan is in each list. Mr Palin deliberately excluded any of his Monty Python colleagues, otherwise Mr Cleese would doubtless have featured.

Michael Palin's
funniest people

1 Peter Cook
2 John Bird
3 George Segal
4 Eric Morecambe
5 Peter Nichols
6 Vladimir Nabokov
7 Evelyn Waugh

8 Spike Milligan
9 Peter Sellers
10 Geoffrey Boycott

Mr Palin's comments: 'Peter Cook undoubtedly. I like George Segal because I like actors who underplay, who don't set out deliberately to make you laugh, whose work you can quietly enjoy. Eric Morecambe has a gift for being verbally very funny, though I can see it might be hard to live with. I like Peter Nichols's plays, especially *The National Health*. Nabokov is so arrogant, but he's very funny. Every sentence is worth reading four times. I like Waugh's confidence. Spike Milligan is in as a Goon, but Sellers is there as an actor. Boycott is not meant as a joke. I genuinely think he is very funny. He produces such a wonderful reaction in other people. He upsets them utterly by being unrelenting and unhelpful. He's very Yorkshire in his public pronouncements. I think he means it all and that he's a man of humour. I'd love to see "The G. Boycott House" on TV.'

Eric Morecambe's
funniest people

1 Terry Cooper – brilliantly funny
2 Ernie Wise – rich and funny
3 Harry Worth – very funny
4 Little and Large – will be very funny
5 Kenny Everett – could be very funny
6 Cannon and Ball – they are very funny
7 Ronnie Barker – is already very funny
8 Marti Caine – oh, she's very funny
9 Two Ronnies – almost funny
10 Everybody else except Bernard Manning.

KINGS AND QUEENS

Longest-reigning
English monarchs

1	Queen Victoria	63 years
2	George III	59 "
3	Henry III	56 "
4	Edward III	50 "
5	Elizabeth I	44 "
6	Henry VI	39 "
7	Henry VIII	38 "
8	Ethelred II	37 "
9	Charles II	36 "
10	Henry I	35 "
11	Edward I	35 "
12	Henry II	35 "
13	George II	33 "

Shortest-reigning
English monarchs

1	Lady Jane Grey	14 days
2	Edward V	75 "
3	Edward VIII	325 "
4	Ethelbald	2 years
5	Hardicanute	2 "
6	Richard III	2 "
7	Edwy	3 "
8	James II	3 "
9	Edward the Martyr	4 "
10	Ethelred I	5 "
11	Harold I	5 "
12	Mary I	5 "

LABOUR WARD

Daily Mail

The most popular cassettes that pregnant ladies at St Thomas's Hospital, London, enjoy during labour.

1 Bruch's Violin Concerto in G minor
2 Theme from *The Sting*
3 West Indian steel band music
4 Reggae
5 Tchaikovsky ballet music
6 Strauss waltzes
7 'Bridge Over Troubled Waters'
8 Abba
9 The Carpenters
10 Current chart-toppers

According to Professor Murdoch Elder, head of Hammersmith Hospital's Obstetrics and Gynaecology Department, between 60 and 70 per cent of mothers opt to have music in the delivery rooms at his hospital. The idea behind it is that music induces relaxation. Music depicting the sea is a favourite; after all, contractions come in waves.

LANGUAGES

Each week the Inner London Education Authority runs 1 941 classes in foreign languages at its various Adult Education Colleges throughout London. Judged by the number of classes laid on for each of the different languages, French is the most popular.

Most popular
foreign languages

	classes per week		*classes per week*
French	594	Japanese	13
German	348	Turkish	13
Spanish	294	Dutch	12
Italian	230	Chinese	11
Bengalese	56	Danish	10
Greek	46	Polish	10
Arabic	44	Irish Gaelic	9
Russian	32	Swedish	8
Finnish	28	Welsh	5
Hebrew	28	Persian	4
Urdu	18	Czech	3
Portuguese	15	Bulgarian	3

LAWYERS

The most frequent reason for consulting a lawyer is for house conveyancing (when purchasing a house), according to a legal survey in 1977 – *The Use of Legal Services in England and Wales*. As percentages, these are the main types of reasons:

1	House conveyance	30%
2	Winding up estates	11%
3	Making and altering wills	10%
4	Divorce	7%
5	Motoring offences	4%
6	Other offences	3%
7	Road traffic injury compensation	3%
8	Industrial injury compensation	3%

The remaining 29% comprised too many kinds of reasons to list.

LEGS

Ernie Wise's
favourite legs

Mr Wise is always being teased by his partner Mr Morecambe about his short fat hairy legs, but in show-business generally his legs have long been admired. Oh, yes. After very long consideration, these are the best legs he himself has ever seen. And he has got a lovely wife.

1 **Mine** – they've always been admired. Even in drag, people tell me how lovely they are, so well-shaped and hairy.

2 **Shirley Bassey's** – she walks beautifully, taking very short steps; minces, I think that's the word. She wears long dresses very tight around the ankle, which help to make her legs look even better.

3 **Angela Rippon's** – I've studied them closely at first hand and they're very, very nice. Such a shame she has to sit behind that desk. I always used to think she used roller skates.

4 **Deirdre Cat's** – she used to be a tennis player. I watched her specially for her legs. Virginia Wade has nice legs, but a bit muscular. Tennis clothes are very good for showing off legs, as are ice-skating clothes and fish-net tights, hmmm.

5 **Nureyev's** – I'd better mention a man, I suppose. It depends what you're looking for in legs. I like feminine legs, personally, but his are good, muscular, well-shaped manly legs.

6 **Miss Dot's** – she was my teacher at primary school, Fitzwilliam School near Hemsworth in Yorkshire. I watched her legs all the time. She had a lovely pair. I came up to her knee-caps at the time.

7 **Geoff Boycott's** – he comes from the same part of Yorkshire but that's not why I've chosen him. He's got very good legs. I can't mention any footballers, as I don't follow football.

8 **Cyd Charisse's** – I have to mention her, even though she's not British. Perfect legs and a perfect body.

9 **Juliet Prowse's** – oh yes, the longest legs I've ever seen.
10 **Eddie Molloy's** – he was the Dame in our pantomime at the Birmingham Hippodrome about ten years ago. Perhaps the really loveliest legs I've ever seen . . . .

PS FOR LEG FANCIERS Were William Wordsworth's legs the worst looking legs ever? This is Thomas de Quincey writing about Wordsworth's legs in the 1830s, and being extremely rude: 'His legs were pointedly condemned by all female connoisseurs in legs; not that they were bad in any way which *would* force itself upon your notice – there was no absolute deformity about them; undoubtedly they had been serviceable legs beyond the average standard of human requisition. I calculate that with these identical legs Wordsworth must have traversed 175 000 English miles. But, useful as they have proved themselves, the Wordsworth legs were certainly not ornamental. A sculptor would certainly have disapproved of their contour. It was a pity, as I agreed with a lady in thinking, that he had not another pair for evening dress wear when no boots lend their friendly aid to mask our imperfections from the eyes of female rigorists . . .'

LEISURE

Leisure activities by social class, 1970

Central Statistical Office

Proportion in each class doing selected activity at least monthly in previous year	Professional & Managerial	Clerical	Skilled	Semi-skilled and un-skilled	All
Home-based activities:		(Percentage)			
Watching television	95	99	98	95	97
Gardening	70	62	66	50	64
Playing with children	59	63	66	59	62
Home decorating/repairs	52	55	56	45	53
Car cleaning	55	44	51	35	48
Playing an instrument	10	8	5	4	7
Total number of home-based activities engaged in at least monthly	5·7	5·9	5·2	4·2	5·3
Sporting activities					
Swimming	34	25	20	8	22
Fishing	9	3	9	5	8
Table tennis	10	10	4	2	6
Sailing	6	—	1	—	2
Other leisure activities					
Going for a drive	62	51	62	49	58
Going to a pub	51	42	54	58	52
Going for a walk	56	63	41	36	47
Going out for a meal	48	31	25	23	32
Attending church	22	20	12	7	15
Total number of leisure activities engaged in at least monthly	3.5	3·3	2·8	2·5	3·0

Watching TV, the most common activity, is indulged on average twenty hours a week by everyone over five years of age.

LIBRARIES

Number of public
libraries
UNESCO and Heron House

	thousands
UK	135·0
Italy	8·7
USA	8·3
W. Germany	2·5
Switzerland	1·9
Belgium	1·6
Spain	1·4
Australia Japan	0·9
France	0·8
Canada	0·7
Norway	0·5
Sweden Netherlands Austria	0·4
Denmark	0·3
Ireland	0·03

Britain hammers the world when it comes to public libraries. Even when the figures are based on numbers per 100 000 of the population, Britain still leads – with 239, followed a long way behind by Switzerland, 29, and Italy and Belgium, 16 each. One explanation is that many of our public libraries are very small. Our librarians, when compiling their figures, cleverly include travelling libraries – i.e. vans – a speciality of our rural areas, which naturally puts up the figures. Nonetheless, it is a remarkable fact that every town of even modest size in the UK has at least one public library, free to all, a record equalled by no other country.

LISTS

A letter from a List Collector, Mrs Louise Gill. Could she be the first in the world to collect shopping lists?

Exeter, Devon.
20 January 1980.

Dear Mr Davies,

In my college days I began a scrapbook of lists, collected on pavements, in library books and on supermarket floors. These lists were mostly shopping lists, probably the lists most often written in everyday life, especially by women. This collection consisted of lists written on various articles, from old Christmas cards to torn-out diary pages. I now have a collection of 60 shopping lists in my scrapbook.

This is the very first list I acquired, found on a café table complete with the biro, in the summer of 1974 at the Princess Pavilion, Falmouth, Cornwall – now called the Tivoli Biergarten. It is certainly an odd mixture of items!

$\frac{1}{2}$ yd orange velvet velcro (green or lilac)
12 lemon squeezers
Body Language bra 36A
Dress
My necklace
Prescription
Bar of Old English Lavender soap
Records
Mincemeat

LITERATURE

The Booker Prize

Inaugurated in 1968, this is the most important and most lucrative annual prize for fiction. It is now worth £10 000 and is sponsored by Booker McConnell Ltd, and administered by the National Book League. The prize is awarded to the best novel, in the opinion of the judges, published each year. The prize is open to novels written in English by citizens of the British Commonwealth, the Republic of Ireland and the Republic of South Africa, and published for the first time in the UK by a British publisher.

1969	*Something to Answer For* by P. H. Newby, published by Faber & Faber
1970	*The Elected Member* by Bernice Rubens, published by Eyre Methuen
1971	*In a Free State* by V. S. Naipaul, published by André Deutsch
1972	*G.* by John Berger, published by Weidenfeld & Nicolson
1973	*The Siege of Krishnapur* by J. G. Farrell, published by Weidenfeld & Nicolson
1974	*The Conservationist* by Nadine Gordimer, published by Jonathan Cape
1975	*Heat and Dust* by Ruth Prawer Jhabvala, published by John Murray
1976	*Saville* by David Storey, published by Jonathan Cape
1977	*Staying On* by Paul Scott, published by William Heinemann
1978	*The Sea, The Sea* by Iris Murdoch, published by Chatto & Windus
1979	*Offshore* by Penelope Fitzgerald, published by Collins

LIVESTOCK

The number of livestock in Britain in June 1979, supplied by the UK Agricultural Supply Trade Association.

Poultry	120 388 000
Sheep	44 446 000
Cattle	13 534 000
Pigs	7 873 000

LONDON

There are thirty-two London Boroughs – twelve of them classed as Inner London Boroughs.

The top ten boroughs in order of population, 1978

1	Croydon	320 800
2	Ealing	292 300
3	Bromley	292 200
4	Barnet	289 900
5	Wandsworth*	275 500
6	Lambeth*	272 300
7	Enfield	259 500
8	Brent	254 900
9	Havering	240 100
10	Lewisham*	240 100

*Inner London Borough

The top ten boroughs in
order of rateable value,
1 April 1979

		£
1	City of Westminster*	305 010 000
2	Camden	104 318 000
3	Kensington and Chelsea*	69 661 000
4	Croydon	66 150 000
5	Barnet	58 000 000
6	Lambeth*	57 743 000
7	Ealing	56 735 000
8	Hillingdon	55 172 000
9	Southwark*	55 000 000
10	Islington*	50 699 000

*Inner London Borough

The best of London Transport

List provided by Ian Farquarson of Richmond

Underground

Longest continuous tunnel: Northern
Line (East Finchley to Morden via Bank)   17 miles 528 yards
Longest journey without change:
Central Line (West Ruislip to Epping)   34·1 miles
Longest distance between adjacent
stations by rail: Metropolitan Line
(Chesham to Chalfont and Latimer)   3·89 miles
Shortest distance between adjacent
stations: Piccadilly Line
(Leicester Square to Covent Garden)   0·16 miles
Most-used stations: Oxford Circus, Victoria, King's Cross,
Piccadilly Circus, Liverpool Street, Baker Street
Station with most platforms: Moorgate
(2 Northern Line, 4 Metropolitan &
Circle Lines, 4 British Rail)   10

Station with most escalators:
Oxford Circus   14
Longest escalator: Leicester Square
(161′ 6″ long on slope with vertical rise
of 80′ 9″)   about 175′ 6″
Deepest station: Hampstead   192′
Deepest lift shaft: Hampstead   181′
Fastest lift: Hampstead   800′ per minute
Highest point above sea level:
Metropolitan Line (West of Amersham
station)   about 500′
Average scheduled speed: 20·4 m.p.h.
Most frequent service: Northern Line – southbound between Kennington and Tooting Broadway at the height of the evening peak hours. Normally 33 trains per hour.

Most-distant places served		*Mileage from Central London*
North-west	Chesham	29
North	Cockfosters	12
	High Barnet	12
North-east	Ongar	24
East	Upminster	18
South	Morden	10
West	Uxbridge	17

The oldest Line: Metropolitan, opened 1863
The newest Line: Jubilee, opened 1979
The latest 'tube' section: Heathrow Central to Hatton Cross, opened 1977

Buses
Points served by the largest number of buses per hour during peak periods: Hyde Park Corner and Trafalgar Square
Longest route: Epping (St Margaret's Hospital) to Brentwood, 23·9 miles
Oldest route: (prior to 1856) Hammersmith to Liverpool Street (now part of Route 9)
First bus service: Paddington to Bank of England, 1829
Largest garages: New Cross and Holloway
Smallest garages: Kingston and Abbey Wood

LUXURIES

The most unusual luxuries
on *Desert Island Discs*

Desert Island Discs is a popular radio programme which has been running for thirty-eight years. In it Roy Plomley asks people to pick their eight favourite gramophone records to take to a desert island. They are also allowed to take one luxury. These are some of the luxuries his guests have chosen in recent years.

1 **Roy Dotrice** – a Dress suit (so he could dress for dinner every evening).

2 **Hermione Gingold** – the Albert Memorial.

3 **Anthony Asquith** – a fully equipped seaside pier, complete with slot machines and What the Butler Saw.

4 **Kiri Te Kanawa** – her collection of kitchen knives. She gives herself a new knife on each new operatic performance.

5 **Sir Michael Tippett** – a Harmonium (it never goes out of tune).

6 **Michael Crawford** – a blow-up rubber woman, plus a puncture repair outfit. [Many guests have chosen a rubber woman over the years, notably Duncan Carse, Oliver Reed, Vincent Brome, Ronnie Scott – but Michael Crawford was the first to add a repair outfit.]

7 **Harry Secombe** – a collapsible concrete model of Broadcasting House with plastic announcers and cast-iron commissionaires so that he could think of all the lads working their nuts off while he lazed in the desert island sun.

8 **Benno Moiseiwitsch** – a roulette wheel (so he could try some new systems).

9 **Sir Clifford Curzon** – a pill to finish himself off with. [Artur Rubenstein also wanted some means of suicide, but chose a revolver.]

10 **Alec Guinness** – an unlimited supply of apricot brandy.

11 **Glenda Jackson** – the Queen's dolls' house to play with.

12 **Frank Muir** – a navel brush, for cleaning his navel.

MARKS & SPENCER

Marks & Spencer's best lines

In an average week, the 252 Marks & Spencer stores in the UK take £30 million. The top ten lines, in order of cash taken, are as follows:

1 Chicken
2 Ladies' jumpers
3 Ladies' skirts
4 Ladies' trousers and jeans
5 Men's trousers and jeans
6 Ladies' dresses
7 Cakes and desserts
8 Men's long-sleeved shirts
9 Ladies' long-sleeved blouses
10 Pies and flans

The reason for the absence of underwear – ladies', men's and children's – in the top ten cash list is that the average unit price is low, around 95p. The average chicken is about £2, so you can sell half as many of them and still beat underwear in terms of cash.

In unit sales, however, underwear would do best. M. & S. sell 100 million pairs of knickers every year, a third of all those bought in the UK.

M. & S. are a bit coy about revealing the individual earnings, except to say that chickens, their cash winner, sell at a rate of half a million birds a week, which means around £1 million a week.

MARRIAGE

Religious and civil ceremonies in Great Britain, 1978

	all marriages (thousands)
Manner of solemnization:	
Church of England/Church in Wales	117
Church of Scotland	15
Roman Catholic Church	34
Other Christian	32
Jews and other non-Christian	1
Register Office	195
Total marriages	394
Percentage of marriages solemnized in Register Offices:	
England and Wales	51
Scotland	38
Great Britain	49

One-third of people marrying for the first time get married in a Register Office. When it comes to subsequent marriages, around four-fifths use a Register Office.

In 1978, over half of the total number of marriages in Great Britain included a person re-marrying, which is reflected in the figure of 49% for all marriages now taking place in Register Offices.

MAZES

Best British mazes

List supplied by Adrian Fisher, maze consultant, of St Albans, Herts

	date created	place	material	size	designer	remarks
1	Earlier than 1670	Hampton Court Palace East Molesey, Surrey	yew	68 × 25m	Unknown	The earliest hedge maze in Britain; receives 1 million visitors a year.
2	c.1670	High Rocks Hotel nr. Tunbridge Wells, Kent	laurel	57 × 21m	Exact copy of Hampton Court Maze	Visited by James II who used to attend the wells.
3	1833	Glandurgan nr. Falmouth, Cornwall	laurel	—	Alfred Fox	Only open on certain days during the summer. Owned by The National Trust.
4	1848	Somerleyton Hall nr. Lowestoft, Suffolk	yew	75 × 49m	William Nesfield	Central Pagoda on top of knoll.
5	1866	Worden Park Leyland, Lancs	beech	—	A member of the Harington family	Worden Hall burnt down in 1943; now the maze is in a public park.
6	1905	Hever Castle nr. Edenbridge, Kent	yew	23 × 23m	William Waldorf Astor	Maze used to recreate the Tudor setting where Henry VIII courted Anne Boleyn.
7	1935	Hazlehead Park Aberdeen	privet	58 × 49m	Sir Henry Alexander?	Given to the citizens of Aberdeen by Sir Henry Alexander.

Continued on next page

	date created	place	material	size	designer	remarks
8	1950	St. Laurence's Rectory Wyck Rissington, Glos.	hawthorn and ivy	25 × 20m	Canon H. S. Cheales	Maze of the Mysteries of the Gospels. More for the pilgrim than the sightseer.
9	1959	Victoria Park Scarborough, North Yorks	privet	41 × 30m	Scarborough Borough Council	—
10	1962	Chatsworth Bakewell, Derbyshire	yew	40 × 35m	D. A. Fisher	On the site of Joseph Paxton's Great Conservatory; design based on earlier maze of First Duke of Devonshire. Floodlit between June and September
11	1962	Blackgang Chine Isle of Wight	privet	27 × 25m	John Dabell	—
12	1963	Esplanade Maze Scarborough, North Yorks	privet	32 × 22m	Scarborough Borough Council	—
13	c. 1930	Tatton Park Knutsford, Cheshire	beech	—	4th Baron, Lord Egerton of Tatton	Maze in good condition and a great feature of the gardens.
14	1978	Longleat House Warminster, Wilts	yew	116 × 54m	Greg Bright	The world's largest maze. Britain's first three-dimensional maze.

MONEY

By the time you read this, wages somewhere will have gone up, but it shows the relative increases in recent years.

Gross weekly earnings of full-time workers in GB

	men £s				
	1970	1975	1976	1977	1978
Manual workers	26·2	54·7	63·9	70·0	79·1
Non-manual workers	34·7	66·8	79·7	86·9	98·5
All workers	29·3	59·5	70·2	76·9	87·1

	women £s				
	1970	1975	1976	1977	1978
Manual workers	13·4	32·1	39·4	43·7	49·4
Non-manual workers	17·8	39·6	48·8	53·8	59·1
All workers	16·3	37·4	46·2	51·0	56·4

MUSIC

Your 100 Best Tunes – the top twenty favourites, 1979

BBC

Your 100 Best Tunes has been broadcast on Sunday nights on Radio 2 for the last twenty-one years, and has one of the highest radio audiences. It was devised by Alan Keith, who also compiles and presents it. A listeners' poll is taken approximately every five years to assess the most popular music. Here Alan Keith lists the top twenty favourite tunes in 1979.

1	In the Depths of the Temple: *The Pearl Fishers*	Bizet
2	The Chorus of the Hebrew Slaves: Nabucco	Verdi
3	*Finlandia*	Sibelius
4	Miserere (King's College, Cambridge)	Allegri
5	Violin Concerto in G Minor	Bruch
6	Symphony No 6	Beethoven
7	Canon in D	Pachelbel
8	Nimrod: *Enigma Variations*	Elgar
9	Intermezzo *Cavalleria Rusticana*	Mascagni
10	'New World' Symphony: *Largo*	Dvorak
11	'Jesu, Joy of Man's Desiring'	Bach
12	Largo (Ombra Mai Fu), *Serse*	Handel
13	'Abide With Me'	W. H. Monk
14	Piano Concerto No 5 ('Emperor')	Beethoven
15	Hallelujah Chorus, *Messiah*	Handel
16	Pomp and Circumstance March No 1	Elgar
17	Ave Verum Corpus	Mozart
18	Arrival of the Queen of Sheba, *Solomon*	Handel
19	Air: Third Suite For Orchestra	Bach
20	Nun's Chorus: *Casanova*	J. Strauss

NAMES

Names which are numbers

George Mell of Tadworth, Surrey, has amused himself for many years by compiling a list of place-names which are also numbers. This is his total so far. He's got names for each number up to twenty, but then, alas, he has a few gaps.

One Man's Pass, Co. Donegal, Eire.
Two Pots, Ilfracombe, Devon.
Three-Legged Cross, Dorset.
Four Throws, Kent.

Fivepenny Borve, Lewis, Hebrides.
Six Bells, Monmouthshire.
Seven Emu River, Australia.
Eightlands, Yorkshire.
Ninestane Rig, Roxburghshire.
Ten Acres, Birmingham.
Eleven Lane Ends, Co. Armagh, Northern Ireland.
Twelveheads, Cornwall.
Twelve Pins, Galway, Eire.
Baker's Dozen Islands, Hudson's Bay, Canada.
Fourteen Streams Station, South Africa.
Fifteen-Mile Falls Dam, Vermont, USA.
Sixteen Island Lake, Quebec, Canada.
Seventeen Mile Creek, Ontario, Canada.
Eighteen Mile Tank, New South Wales, Australia.
Nineteen Mile Creek, British Columbia, Canada.
Twenty, Lincolnshire.
Twenty-four Parganas, West Bengal, India.
Twenty Six, Kentucky, USA.
Twentynine Palms, Mojave Desert, California, USA.
Thirty-one Mile Lake, Quebec, Canada.
Treinta y Tres (Spanish for 33), Uruguay.
Trentanove (Italian for 39), Mediterranean islet.
Forty Foot Bridge, Huntingdonshire.
Eight and Forty, Yorkshire.
Fifty Six, Stone County, Arizona, USA.
Sixty Mile River, Alaska.
Seventy Mile House, British Columbia, Canada.
Ninety Mile Beach, Victoria, Australia.
Ninety Six, South Carolina, USA.
Hundred House, Radnorshire, Wales.
Seven Score, Kent.
Thousand Oaks, California, USA.
Ten Thousand Smokes, Alaska.

'My 1 to 20 sequence was destroyed in May 1968 when the Thirteen Arches railway viaduct, near Bristol, was blown up to make way for the M32, but I soon filled the gap with an acceptable 13 – Baker's Dozen Islands.

'Many numbers still elude me but I have lots of duplicates such as Three Bridges, Five Elms, Thousand Islands International Bridge (Ontario), Nine Mile Ride, Tenino (Washington, USA), Four Mile Bridge, Two Mile Hill, Sixmile Bridge (one in Northumberland and another in Co. Clare), Fifteen Arch Bridge, Forty Fork (Pennsylvania, USA), Ten Thousand Islands (Florida, USA), Six Towns (Londonderry) and several more.

'I'm still hoping to fill the many gaps in the above list.'

NATIONAL GALLERY

Top Postcards

The National Gallery sells an average of 1¾ million postcards per year. These were the top selling ones as of January, 1980.

1	The Leonardo Cartoon	37 000
2	Renoir: *Les Parapluies*	25 000
3	Monet: *The Thames Below Westminster*	22 000
4	Constable: *The Hay Wain*	19 000
5	Van Gogh: *Sunflowers*	17 000
6	Turner: *The Fighting Temeraire*	16 000
7	Van Gogh: *A Cornfield with Cypresses*	15 500
8	Van Eyck: *The Marriage of Giovanni*	14 000
9	Renoir: *The Cabaret*	13 500
10	Monet: *The Water-Lily Pond*	12 000

The Leonardo Cartoon, at 37 000, has been the number one seller for almost twenty years now, but Monet's *The Thames Below Westminster*, which sold 22 000, is coming up fast, considering it has only been in the Gallery around six years. Drouais's *Madame de Pompadour*, acquired by the National Gallery in 1979, sold 2 500 in three months and is obviously the one to watch for the future. People buy a postcard because they've just seen and liked the original – regardless of how the postcards are arranged on the bookstall. If a painting is moved to a less prominent wall, postcard sales drop immediately.

NATIONAL PARKS

There are now ten National Parks in England and Wales, areas of national beauty and importance which were designated as such and given certain legal safeguards under a 1949 Act. They now cover 9% of the land surface.

The idea came from the USA. Most European countries had them years before England and Wales; Scotland still has none.

National Parks in
England and Wales – in acres

(date of origin in brackets)

1	Lake District (17 April 1951)	554 240
2	Snowdonia (18 October 1951)	540 800
3	Yorkshire Dales (12 October 1954)	435 200
4	North Yorkshire Moors (28 November 1952)	353 920
5	Peak District (17 April 1951)	346 880
6	Brecon Beacons (17 April 1957)	332 160
7	Northumberland (6 April 1956)	254 720
8	Dartmoor (30 October 1951)	233 600
9	Exmoor (19 October 1954)	169 600
10	Pembrokeshire (29 February 1952)	144 000

NICKNAMES FOR THE PM

Mrs Thatcher has been known by many names, but alas some are not repeatable in a family book.

Snatcher
The Iron Maiden
HM
Her Majesty
The Boss
That Woman
Gloriana
The Mekon
Attila the Hen

NOBEL PRIZES: BRITISH WINNERS

Six prizes are awarded each year in chemistry, economics, literature, peace, physics and physiology or medicine. The first prizes were awarded in 1901 – the economics prize was added in 1969.

Chemistry

1904	Sir William Ramsay
1908	Ernest Rutherford
1921	Frederick Soddy
1922	Francis W. Aston
1929	Arthur Harden*
1937	Walter N. Haworth*
1947	Sir Robert Robinson

*shared prize

1952	Archer J. P. Martin
	Richard L. M. Synge
1956	Sir Cyril N. Hinshelwood★
1957	Lord Todd (Alexander K. Todd)
1958	Frederick Sanger
1962	Sir John C. Kendrew
	Max F. Perutz
1964	Dorothy Crowfoot Hodgkin
1967	Ronald G. W. Norrish
	Sir George Porter★
1969	Derek H. R. Barton★
1973	Geoffrey Wilkinson★
1975	John W. Cornforth★
1978	Peter Mitchell

Economics

1972	Sir John K. Hicks★
1977	James Edward Meade★
1979	Sir Arthur Lewis

Literature

1907	Rudyard Kipling
1925	George Bernard Shaw
1932	John Galsworthy
1948	T. S. Eliot
1950	Bertrand Russell
1953	Sir Winston Churchill

★shared prize

Medicine

1902	Sir Ronald Ross
1922	Archibald V. Hill*
1929	Sir Frederick G. Hopkins*
1932	Edgar D. Adrian
	Sir Charles S. Sherrington
1936	Sir Henry H. Dale*
1945	Sir Alexander Fleming
	Ernst B. Chain
	Sir Howard W. Florey
1953	Hans A. Krebs
1960	Peter B. Medawar*
1962	Francis H. C. Crick*
	Maurice H. F. Wilkins
1963	Alan L. Hodgkin
	Andrew F. Huxley
1970	Bernard Katz*
1972	Rodney Porter*
1973	Nikolas Tinbergen*
1979	Godfrey Hounsfield*

Peace

1903	Sir William R. Cremer
1925	Sir J. Austen Chamberlain*
1933	Sir Norman Angell
1934	Arthur Henderson
1937	Viscount Cecil of Chelwood
1947	Friends Service Council*
1949	Lord John Boyd Orr of Brechin
1959	Philip J. Noel-Baker
1976	Betty Williams & Mairead Lorrigan

*shared prize

Physics

*shared prize

FAMOUS NON-GRADUATES

Politicians, intellectuals, authors and such like whom you might expect to have been to university . . .

James Callaghan, Prime Minister
Joseph Chamberlain, statesman
Winston Churchill, Prime Minister
Joseph Conrad, novelist
Benjamin Disraeli, Prime Minister
Sir James Goldsmith, businessman
Rudyard Kipling, author

David Lloyd George, Prime Minister
Lord Olivier, actor
Lord Ritchie-Calder, Professor, Edinburgh University (1961–7)
George Bernard Shaw, playwright
Tom Stoppard, playwright
Virginia Woolf, author

OLYMPIC GAMES

Total number of medals won
at summer Olympic Games 1896–1976

International Olympic Committee archives

USA	1514½	Switzerland	156
Russia*	670	Denmark	137½
UK	526½	Netherlands	133
W. Germany	494½	Belgium	126
France	449	Canada	122
Sweden	401	Norway	101
Italy	345	Austria	79
Japan	200	Ireland	13
E. Germany**	181	Spain	11
Australia	178		

* Russia only competed 11 times out of 19 games
** E. Germany only competed 3 times out of 19 games
½ = tie with other country

Winter sports

Britain has won only fifteen individual or team medals in the
Winter Olympic Games since the first Winter Games in 1908.
The winners were:

gold
1936	Ice hockey team
1952	Jeanette Altwegg (figure skating, women)

128

1964	Two-man bobsleigh team (Tony Nash, Robin Dixon)
1976	John Curry (figure skating, men)
1980	Robin Cousins (figure skating, men)

silver

| 1908 | Phyllis and James Johnson (figure skating, pairs) |
| 1936 | Cecilia Colledge (figure skating, women) |

bronze

1908	Dorothy Greenhough-Smith (figure skating, women)
1908	Madge and Edgar Syers (figure skating, pairs)
1924	Ethel Muckelt (figure skating, women)
1924	Ice hockey team
1928	Lord Northesk (skeleton toboggan)
1936	Four-man bobsleigh team (F. McEvoy, J. Cardno, G. Dugdale, C. Green)
1948	Jeanette Altwegg (figure skating, women)
1948	John Crammond (skeleton toboggan)

OPERATIONS

Most frequent types of surgical operations in England and Wales

Reproduced with the permission of the Controller of HMSO

This list of the most frequently performed categories of surgical operations is based on the 1976 Hospital In-Patient Enquiry. This annual Enquiry is based on a one in ten sample of discharges from NHS (non-psychiatric) hospitals in England and Wales, and organized by the DHSS, the Office of Population Censuses and the Welsh Office.

A surgical operation is defined as any therapeutic or major diagnostic procedure which involves the use of instruments or the manipulation of part of the body and generally takes place under operating theatre conditions.

Operation	Estimated number
1 **Obstetrics** (which includes ante-natal and post-natal operations as well as assisted births)	446 830
2 **Abdominal** (which includes hernia, appendix, colon, gall bladder)	420 840
3 **Female genital organs**	294 560
4 **Orthopaedic** (fractures and operations on joints)	231 880
5 **Ear, nose and throat**	213 690
6 **Urinary system**	118 170
7 **Skin**	96 900
8 **Eye**	96 900
9 **Male genital organs**	91 350
10 **Upper alimentary tract** (teeth, jaw)	76 010

Most frequent individual surgical operations

There are 999 different operations, each with its own name and number, as listed by the Department of Health. These were the most frequently performed in 1976.

Operation	Estimated number
1 **Episiotomy** (assisted birth)	194 100
2 **Curettage of uterus**	118 400
3 **Repair of inguinal hernia**	67 550
4 **Cystoscopy** (bladder)	65 630
5 **Emergency appendicectomy** (removal of the appendix)	59 560
6 **Termination of pregnancy**	52 760

7 **Removal of retained products**	51 510
(post-natal or post-abortion)	
8 **Tonsillectomy with adenoidectomy**	51 260
(removal of the tonsils and adenoids)	
9 **Forceps delivery**	49 190
10 **Cholecystectomy**	39 470
(removal of the gall bladder)	

Normal delivery, which does not count as surgical, came to 240 370 – the most frequent single reason for people going into hospital.

OUTDOOR ACTIVITIES

Membership of organizations

	1978
Camping	*thousands*
Camping Club of Great Britain and Ireland	178
Caravan Club	193
Walking, climbing and riding	
Youth Hostels Association (including	
Scottish YHA)	316
Ramblers' Association	29
British Horse Society	27
The Pony Club	50
British Mountaineering Council	38
British Orienteering Federation	5
Water Sports	
British Canoe Union	9
Royal Yachting Association	57
British Sub-Aqua Club	28

Cycling
British Cycling Federation | 16
Cyclists Touring Club | 32

Flying
British Gliding Association | 11
(Current private pilot licences issued | 23)

Miscellaneous
National Trust (including NT for Scotland) | 861
English Golf Union | 460
British Field Sports Society | 47

OXFORD COLLEGES IN ORDER OF FOUNDATION

University	1249	Pembroke	1624
Balliol	1263	Worcester	1714
Merton	1264	Keble	1868
St Edmund Hall	1270	Hertford	1874
Exeter	1314	Lady Margaret Hall	1878
Oriel	1326	Somerville	1879
Queen's	1340	St Hugh's	1886
New College	1379	Mansfield	1886
Lincoln	1427	St Hilda's	1893
All Souls	1438	St Peter's	1929
Magdalen	1458	Nuffield	1937
Brasenose	1509	St Antony's	1950
Corpus Christi	1517	St Anne's	1952
Christ Church	1546	Linacre	1962
Trinity	1554	St Catherine's	1962
St John's	1555	St Cross	1965
Jesus	1571	Wolfson	1965
Wadham	1612	Green	1979

PAIN

Don't read this list. It might give you a headache...

Percentage of population (men and women) who suffer regularly from headaches, 1977

Heron House

UK ⎫ Spain ⎭	42
Belgium	40
France ⎫ Italy ⎭	39
Netherlands	38
Austria ⎫ Switzerland ⎭	36
Denmark	34
Norway	31
W. Germany	28
Sweden	27
USA	13

PAINTINGS

Sotheby's world record prices for individual artists, 1979

1 **Frederick Edwin Church** *Icebergs*, a painting which had hung in a private home in Manchester since 1861, its whereabouts unknown to the art world: £1 168 224, the second highest price ever paid for a painting.

2 **Man Ray** *A l'Heure de l'Observatoires: les Amoreux*: £360 576, a record price for any surrealist painting

3 **Max Ernst** *Le Surrealisme et la Peinture*: £298 076

4 **Auguste Rodin** *Jean d'Aire* – nude study for the monument *Les Bourgeois de Calais*, c. 1886: £117 977

5 **John Singleton Copley** Portrait of George Boone Roupell: £110 000

6 **Gustave Moreau** *Saint Sebastian and the Angel*, c. 1876: £80 000

7 **Edvard Munch** *Madonna-Liebendes Weib* – lithograph, printed in black and hand-coloured with gouache: £55 000

8 **Sir Edward Burne-Jones** Two gouaches – *The Sleep of King Arthur in Avalon* and *The Star of Bethlehem*: £30 000 each

9 **Walter Richard Sickert** *The Camden Town Murder or What Shall We Do For The Rent*: £23 500

10 **Laurence Stephen Lowry** *Industrial Landscape*, 1955: £16 500

11 **Arthur Rackham** Ink and watercolour drawing depicting humorous characters and incidents at the seaside, and captioned below 'Common Objects at the Seaside by our Goblinesque Artists. Studies for Goblin Tapestry for Punch's Almanack': £5 200

12 **Eric Kennington** An illustration for the *Seven Pillars of Wisdom* of the Sherif Ali ibn el Hussein – pastel on grey paper: £4 300

13 **John Piper** Watercolour – *The Great Courtyard with the entrance wing and belfry, Montegufoni*: £2 800

Not to be outdone, Christie's also had a very good year in 1979. By January 1980 they held three out of the first four world records for paintings.

Christie's world record prices for individual artists

1 **Velázquez** *Portrait of Juan de Pareja,* a world record price for any picture or work of art. Now in the Metropolitan Museum, New York. Sold in 1970. Fetched £42 when sold on behalf of Sir William Hamilton in 1801. Sir William brought back the picture on board Nelson's flagship with Emma when he was forced to flee from Naples, where he was First Minister, because of the advance of the French: £2 310 000

2 **Titian** *The Death of Actaeon* – the third highest price paid in the world for any painting. It is now in the National Gallery, London: £1 680 000

3 **Duccio** *Crucifixion.* The fourth highest price paid in the world: £1 000 000

4 **Rembrandt** *Titus*: £798 000

5 **Matisse** *Le Jeune Marin 1.* The highest price paid for a post-Impressionist work: £720 000

6 **Monet** *La Terrasse à Sainte Adresse* – a record auction price for the artist: £588 000

7 **Toulouse Lautrec** *La Grande Loge*: £370 000

8 **Mondrian** *Large Composition with Red, Blue and Yellow*: £400 000

9 **David Hockney** *Blue Interior and Two Still Lifes*: £37 000

PAINTS

Best-selling paint colours

Every quarter, ICI Paints Division compiles its own table of the best-selling Dulux paints according to colour. These are

135

the top five throughout the first half of 1979 according to shop sales.

Dulux Gloss	Dulux Vinyl Matt Emulsion
1 Brilliant White	1 Brilliant White
2 Magnolia	2 Magnolia
3 Black	3 Muffin
4 Spice	4 Buttermilk
5 Muffin	5 Early Dawn

There is little regional variation in the popularity of colours and the above list, with the orange-brown 'family' being predominant, has been much the same for three years. (Magnolia, Muffin, Spice and Early Dawn are all classed as members of the brown 'family'.) But Jack Widgery, ICI's Colour Co-ordinator, suspects that brown will have only another year to run. 'There have been signs that the orange-browns are going and that darker, more autumnal chestnut browns are coming in. I think that in 1981 these autumnal browns will change into reds. The whole range of red has been dead for years. Pink, especially, has been dead, colourwise, but I can see signs that pink is beginning to climb and eventually I think it will join the reds. The green "family" is stationary. It's been the second-string colour "family" for years, and I think it will stay there.'

PARLIAMENT

The ten highest majorities in the May 1979 General Election

1 J. H. Molyneaux (O.U.P. Antrim S.)		38 368
2 E. L. Gardner (C. Fyldes)		32 247
3 W. P. Grieve (C. Solihull)		32 207

4	Rt. Hon. T. A. Jones (Lab. Rhondda)	31 481
5	R. M. Marshall (C. Arundel)	30 760
6	Hon. A. G. Hamilton (C. Epsom and Ewell)	26 358
7	Rt. Hon. P. A. Fowler (C. Sutton Coldfield)	26 107
8	I. R. E. Gow (C. Eastbourne)	26 084
9	A. Woodall (Lab. Hemsworth)	26 043
10	P. Hardy (Lab. Rother Valley)	26 002

C.   Conservative
Lab. Labour
O.U.P. Official Unionist Party

The ten smallest majorities
in the General Election

1	R. J. Atkins (C. Preston N.)	29
2	F. R. White (Lab. Bury and Radcliffe)	38
3	P. Robinson (D.U.P. Belfast E.)	64
4	G. R. Cryer (Lab. Keighley)	78
5	J. D. Wheeler (C. Paddington)	106
6	Rt. Hon. S. C. Silkin (Lab. Dulwich)	122
7	J. B. L. Cadbury (C. Northfield)	204
8	P. Whitehead (Lab. Derby N.)	214
9	J. R. Carlisle (C. Luton W.)	246
10	J. H. Aspinwall (C. Kingswood)	303

C.   Conservative
Lab. Labour
D.U.P. Democratic Unionist Party

This next list shows the age and sex of MPs in May 1979 and their occupation at that time. The age distribution has changed little since the October 1974 general election but the present Parliament has only nineteen women MPs compared to twenty-seven previously. The majority of MPs continue to be professional or other non-manual workers: 433 have a university education; 230 were educated at public schools. (See also H for Heaviest MPs.)

Age, sex and occupation of MPs, May 1979

Social Trends

	Labour	Conserv- ative	Liberal	other	total
Age groups:					
Under 40	55	84	3	4	146
41–60	170	217	6	10	403
Over 60	43	38	2	3	86
Total	268	339	11	17	635
of which: men	257	331	11	17	616
women	11	8	0	0	19
Occupations					
Barristers, solicitors	31	70	0	2	103
Journalists, publishers and public relations officers	19	38	1	1	59
Doctors, surgeons	5	3	0	0	8
Teachers, lecturers	53	14	3	4	74
Farmers, landowners	2	25	2	1	30
*Company directors, managers & other business positions	62	193	4	3	262
Engineers	30	8	1	0	39
Trades Union officials	27	1	0	0	28
Other non-manual workers	13	23	0	4	40
Manual workers	32	0	0	2	34

*Some MPs have two or three professions and are included more than once.

The best speakers in the House of Commons

It is a matter of opinion who are the best speakers in Parliament, but according to a straw poll among leading parliamentary experts, these are the five MPs, in order, who are most likely to fill up the Chamber when it is known they are going to speak, though each can have his off day and be extremely boring.

1 Neil Kinnock
2 Enoch Powell
3 Edward Heath
4 Peter Shore
5 Michael Foot

PERSONAL PROBLEMS

Marje Proops has been answering personal problems in the *Daily Mirror* for twenty-five years. These are the eleven most common subjects on which she receives letters:

1 *Matrimonial problems*
Sexual incompetence, unable to have orgasm, premature ejaculation, poor technique: 'My husband is sleeping with another woman . . .', 'My husband is sleeping with another man . . .', 'My wife has a lover . . .'

2 *Loneliness*
Lonely widows and widowers: 'I was married for thirty-seven years and my husband recently died, I'm heartbroken . . .'
Lonely temporarily: wives who are married to long-distance lorry drivers, sailors, men serving overseas, workers on oil rigs, etc.
Lonely teenagers: 'I can't relate to other young people . . .', 'I'm shy and I blush easily . . .'

3 *Jealousy*
Especially common among young unmarried people: 'My girlfriend is so jealous and possessive that I feel trapped . . .', 'My boyfriend hits the roof if I dance with or talk to another bloke at parties . . .'

4 *Teenage problems*

Mostly to do with sex: 'I have an inexperienced young lover . . .'
Contraception: 'Shall I go on the Pill? . . .'
Pleas for help: 'How can I get this boy to love me? . . .'
Resentful of prying mothers who read diaries, look for contraceptives or read private letters.
Rebellion against parents – mothers write saying they can't control their children: 'My daughter is hanging around with a bunch of undesirables . . .'

5 *In-laws*

Mother-in-law jealous of daughter-in-law and vice versa: 'My mother-in-law is always interfering . . .', 'My daughter-in-law is inadequate in bringing up my son's child . . .' Lots of complicated problems relating to children and grandparents.

6 *Homosexuals, transvestites, transexuals*

Ms Proops labelled these all together. One way or another, they see themselves as misfits: 'I have a very nice relationship with my flat-mate but my mother worries terribly . . .', 'Father threw me down the stairs because he discovered I was gay and has now thrown me out of the house . . .', 'Am I a freak? . . .'

7 *Depression*

Menopausal problems, pre-menstrual tension, post-natal depression, depression as a result of bereavement, after a hysterectomy operation.

8 *Physical appearance*

'My boobs are too big . . .', 'My boobs are too small . . .', 'My nose is too big, how much will it cost to have plastic surgery? . . .' Noses and boobs are the most common problems concerning appearance.
Anorexia nervosa – girls who have slimmers' disease.

9 *Agoraphobia*

'Help, I'm scared to go out of the house, what can I do? . . .' 'My husband doesn't understand when I say I'm scared to go to the shops . . .'

10 *Unmarried mothers*

Either they're pregnant and want an abortion or they want to get the child adopted: 'I don't know where to go for help . . .', 'I'm pregnant by a married man . . .', 'I told my boyfriend I

was two months' pregnant and he doesn't want to know . . .'
From fourteen-, fifteen- and sixteen-year-olds: 'I can't tell
my mother I'm pregnant . . .'

11 *Employment*

Jobs, careers, promotion, exploitation, pay conditions, bad-tempered colleagues, difficult bosses.

'The types of problems people have are changing as society is changing. The biggest change I've seen in the last twenty-five years or so is the change in the status of women, which creates all kinds of problems. They are demanding equality and independence – quite rightly – but it is putting their marriages and family lives at risk. This in turn affects men – a lot feel insecure and still more feel bloody resentful.

'Most of my letters are from women. They're much more ready with their emotions. After all, boys are taught not to cry and always to keep that stiff upper lip and to a great degree old attitudes and standards are maintained. But I'm receiving more letters from men – about 35% – some of whom really spill their emotions. I got a 72-page letter from a man the other day.'

Marje receives on average approximately 25 000 – 30 000 letters a year. There is a lull in correspondence during the Christmas and summer holidays. After the summer hols there is a marked increase in pregnancies. 'I didn't take the Pill while I was away', 'I went to bed with a Spanish waiter because he promised to love me forever', etc.

There is always a drop in mail when the postal cost increases, but when people get used to paying the extra, the problems flood in again.

POETS LAUREATE

1 John Dryden, 1668–88
2 Thomas Shadwell, 1688–92
3 Nahum Tate, 1692–1715

POP MUSIC

The top-best-selling singles
in the UK since 1960

Record Business

1 'Mull of Kintyre', Wings (1977)
2 'Rivers of Babylon', Boney M (1978)
3 'You're the One That I Want', John Travolta and Olivia Newton John (1978)
4 'Mary's Boy Child', Boney M (1978)
5 'She Loves You', The Beatles (1963)
6 'I Wanna Hold Your Hand', The Beatles (1963)
7 'Tears', Ken Dodd (1965)
8 'Summer Nights', John Travolta and Olivia Newton John (1978)
9 'Can't Buy Me Love', The Beatles (1964)
10 'I Feel Fine', The Beatles (1964)
11 'The Carnival Is Over', The Seekers (1965)

12 'We Can Work It Out'/'Day Tripper', The Beatles (1965)
13 'Bright Eyes', Art Garfunkel (1979)
14 'Y.M.C.A.', Village People (1979)
15 'Bohemian Rhapsody', Queen (1975)
16 'Please Release Me', Engelbert Humperdinck (1967)
17 'It's Now Or Never', Elvis Presley (1960)
18 'Heart of Glass', Blondie (1979)
19 'Green Green Grass of Home', Tom Jones (1966)
20 'I Love You, Love Me', Gary Glitter (1973)

The Beatles monopolize the chart with five singles, and Paul McCartney tops it with the two-million seller 'Mull of Kintyre'. But Ken Dodd managed to outsell the Beatles in 1965 when 'Tears' was released. Boney M put the only Christmas single in the Top Twenty with 'Mary's Boy Child', first made popular by Harry Belafonte – a song written by Jester Hairston who played the butler in *In the Heat of the Night*.

Single sales peaked in 1964 thanks to the Beatles and the Mersey boom, when 73 million singles were sold. The market declined in 1969 with the lowest sales figures of 47 million. With the emergence of punk and disco music singles began to rise again for a while, but they declined in 1979.

It is interesting to note that groups like Abba and The Stones failed to make the list as they haven't *sold a million copies* of any one single.

The top ten albums
of the Seventies
British Research Market Bureau

1 'Bridge Over Troubled Water', Simon and Garfunkel
2 Abba's 'Greatest Hits'
3 'Tubular Bells', Mike Oldfield
4 Simon and Garfunkel's 'Greatest Hits'
5 'Saturday Night Fever', The Bee Gees

6 'The Singles 1969–73', The Carpenters
7 'Arrival', Abba
8 'Dark Side of the Moon', Pink Floyd
9 Original soundtrack from *Grease*
10 Elvis Presley's '40 Greatest Hits'

The most popular albums, 1979
Melody Maker

Coming more up to date, these were the best-selling pop albums in 1979. It remains to be seen how many, if any, become all-time best-sellers.

1 'Parallel Lines', Blondie
2 'Breakfast in America', Supertramp
3 'Discovery', Electric Light Orchestra
4 'Outlandos D'Amour', Police
5 'I Am', Earth Wind and Fire
6 'Voulez-Vous', Abba
7 'Spirits Having Flown', Bee Gees
8 'Armed Forces', Elvis Costello
9 'Replicas', Tubeway Army
10 'Manifesto', Roxy Music

Worst records ever

Kenny Everett, the well-known TV and radio person, asks his listeners on Capital Radio to send him their very worst records, so that he can play them, then smash them. In 1978 a total of 3 210 listeners wrote in – these are the worst records in order of nominations cast.

1 'I Want my Baby Back', Jimmy Cross   510
2 'Wunderbar', Zarah Leander   506
3 'Paralyzed', The Legendary
  Stardust Cowboy   310

Just to show you what a nice person cuddly Ken really is, here are his own favourite tunes.

Kenny Everett's favourites

1 Tchaikovsky's March from Pathétique Symphony
2 Brahms's Violin Concerto in D, opus 77
3 Bizet's Symphony in C, 4th Movement
4 'Steppin' Out' (from 'Out of the Blue' by ELO)
5 'Big Wheels' (from 'Out of the Blue' by ELO)
6 'Sweet is the Night' (from 'Out of the Blue' by ELO)
7 'I'd Rather Leave While I'm in Love', Carole Bayer Sager
8 'Blue Suede Shoes', Elvis Presley
9 Mendelssohn's Violin Concerto in E minor
10 'Strawberry Fields Forever', The Beatles

POPULATION: UK

	millions		*projections*
1901	38·2	1981	55·9
1911	42·1	1986	56·3
1921	44·0	1991	57·0
1931	46·0	1996	57·7
1941	48·2	2001	58·0
1951	50·5		
1961	53·0		
1971	55·7		
1978	55·9		

Population of English counties

(For the size of the counties see 'A' for Acreage.)

Greater London	6 918 100
West Midlands	2 711 600
Greater Manchester	2 663 500
Yorkshire, West	2 067 900

Merseyside	1 545 500
Hampshire	1 453 400
Kent	1 449 000
Essex	1 435 600
Lancashire	1 369 600
Yorkshire, South	1 304 100
Tyne and Wear	1 165 100
Staffordshire	997 000
Surrey	995 400
Nottinghamshire	973 700
Devonshire	948 000
Hertfordshire	947 100
Avon	921 900
Cheshire	919 800
Derbyshire	896 200
Humberside	844 900
Leicestershire	833 300
Norfolk	679 800
Berkshire	672 600
Yorkshire, North	661 300
Sussex, East	652 500
Sussex, West	633 600
Hereford and Worcestershire	610 100
Durham	603 800
Suffolk	592 700
Dorset	586 500
Cambridgeshire	570 200
Cleveland	568 200
Oxfordshire	540 600
Lincolnshire	530 100
Buckinghamshire	525 100
Northamptonshire	516 400
Wiltshire	516 200
Gloucestershire	495 300
Bedfordshire	494 700
Cumbria	472 400
Warwickshire	469 500
Cornwall	416 700
Somerset	411 100

Shropshire	365 900
Northumberland	289 200
Isle of Wight	114 300

Top ten English counties
in order of population density

		people per acre
1	Greater London	17·72
2	West Midlands	12·20
3	Merseyside	9·67
4	Tyne and Wear	8·73
5	Greater Manchester	8·39
6	Yorkshire, West	4·10
7	Cleveland	3·94
8	Yorkshire, South	3·38
9	Avon	2·77
10	Hertfordshire	2·35

Bottom ten English counties
in order of population density

		people per acre
1	Northumberland	0·23
2	Cumbria	0·28
3	Yorkshire, North	0·32
4	Lincolnshire	0·36
5	Shropshire	0·42
6	Cornwall	0·48
	Somerset	0·48
8	Norfolk	0·51
9	Devonshire	0·57
10	Wiltshire	0·60

Population of the largest conurbations, cities and towns, mid-1971

conurbations	*thousands*
Greater London	7 441
South-east Lancashire	2 400
West Midlands	2 371
Yorkshire, West	1 736
Central Clydeside	1 723
Merseyside	1 264
Tyneside	803

cities and towns	
Birmingham	1 014
Glasgow	894
Liverpool	605
Manchester	546
Sheffield	518
Leeds	502
Edinburgh	453
Bristol	426
Teesside	395
Belfast	360
Coventry	334
Nottingham	298
Bradford	294
Kingston upon Hull	285
Leicester	282
Cardiff	277
Wolverhampton	269
Stoke-on-Trent	265
Plymouth	246
Newcastle upon Tyne	221
Derby	219
Sunderland	216
Southampton	213
Portsmouth	205

Population density:
an international comparison

Social Trends

	number of people per sq km 1978
Netherlands	384
Belgium	321
Japan	311
W. Germany	247
UK	229
India	210
Italy	188
Philippines	155
Denmark	119
France	97
Irish Republic	59
Kenya	26
USA	23
Sweden	18
Brazil	14
USSR	12
Canada	2

PREVIOUS NAMES

People born with different names from the ones they later became famous with.

Josef Teodor Konrad Korzeniowski – Joseph Conrad
Archibald Leach – Cary Grant
Eric Arthur Blair – George Orwell
Richard Jenkins – Richard Burton
Bernard Vinogradsky – Lord Delfont

Harry Webb – Cliff Richard
Reg Dwight – Elton John
Maurice Cole – Kenny Everett
Richard Starkey – Ringo Starr
Priscilla White – Cilla Black
Eric Bartholomew – Eric Morecambe
Cecily Isabel Fenwick – Dame Rebecca West
Lesley Hornby – Twiggy
Bob Davis – Jasper Carrott
Margaret Hookham – Margot Fonteyn
Alice Marks – Alicia Markova
Diana Fluck – Diana Dors
Thomas Hicks – Tommy Steele
Maurice Micklewhite – Michael Caine
Leslie Stainer – Leslie Howard
William Mitchell – Peter Finch
Michael Dumble-Smith – Michael Crawford

PRICES

In 1979, food prices increased on average by 11·63% over the previous twelve months compared with 6% in 1978. On the whole, the price of fresh foods increased the most, by 16·58%, while processed foods moved ahead on average 8%. The figures come from *The Grocer*, 12 January 1980.

The top twenty price rises during 1979

1	Eggs	32·07%
2	Vegetables	21·93%
3	Meat	17·85%
4	Frozen meats	15·17%
5	Milk, canned or powdered	14·75%
6	Milk, fresh	13·49%

7	Sugar	13·21%
8	Breakfast cereals	13·20%
9	Canned cream	12·64%
10	Butter	12·56%
11	Cakes	12·44%
12	Cheese	12·32%
13	Frozen vegetables	11·98%
14	Bread	11·59%
15	Biscuits	10·98%
16	Soups	10·49%
17	Canned meats	9·71%
18	Marmalade	7·79%
19	Frozen fish	7·65%
20	Other cereals	7·48%

There were, surprisingly, two commodities which fell in price:
1	Coffee	−7·28%
2	Tea	−2·29%

PSEUDONYMS

Some well-known British writers – and their real names.

George Eliot – Mary Ann Evans
Boz – Charles Dickens
Currer Bell – Charlotte Brontë
Michael Angelo Titmarsh – William Makepeace Thackeray
Silus Tomkyn Comberbacke – S. T. Coleridge
Elia – Charles Lamb
Saki – Hector Hugh Munro
Michael Innes – John I. M. Stewart
John Le Carré – David Cornwell
Nicholas Blake – Cecil Day Lewis
'B. B.' – Denys Watkins-Pitchford

PUBS

Inn Signs, Cadbury Lamb

Most popular pub names

According to a survey carried out by G. W. Shearn of Northampton, who recorded 19 000 British inn names, these are the most frequently used.

1 THE RED LION 386
2 THE CROWN 350
3 THE WHITE HART 269
4 THE NEW INN 234
5 THE KING'S HEAD 178
6 THE KING'S ARMS 159
7 THE ROYAL OAK 151

Football pubs

Pubs which take their names from local football teams.

THE GUNNERS: Finsbury Park, London (Arsenal)
THE SPURS: Edmonton (Tottenham Hotspur)
THE HAPPY WANDERER: Bolton (Bolton Wanderers)
THE SAINTS: Southampton
UNITED: Ashton New Road, Manchester (Manchester United)
THE SKY BLUE: Coundon Green, Coventry (Coventry City)

Unusual pub names

THE SNOOTY FOX: Tetbury, Gloucestershire
THE ELEPHANT'S NEST: Tavistock, Devon
THE BLUE MONKEY: Plymouth, Devon
THE CAT AND CUSTARD POT: Shipton Moyne, Wiltshire

THE DRUNKEN DUCK: Barngate, Cumbria
THE THREE PICKERELS: Mepal, Cambridgeshire
THE SILENT WHISTLE: Evercreech, Somerset
THE SILENT WOMAN: Cold Harbour, Dorset
THE HEADLESS WOMAN: Duddon, Cheshire
THE HONEST LAWYER: King's Lynn, Norfolk
THE CUCKOO BUSH: Gotham, Nottinghamshire
THE WALTZING WEASEL: Birch Vale, Hayfield, Derbyshire
DOFF COCKERS: Bolton, Lancashire
THE FINNYGOOK: Crafthole, Cornwall
THE SCROGG: Newcastle upon Tyne
RHUBARB: Bristol
SACK OF POTATOES: Gosta Green, Birmingham
CUSTARD HOUSE: Small Heath, Birmingham
THE STORK AT REST: Stacey Close, Gravesend, Kent
THE STARVING RASCAL: Amblecote, West Midlands
BUNCH OF CARROTS: Hampton Bishop, Hereford
THE QUEEN'S HEAD AND ARTICHOKE: London

QUIZZES

Top of the Form is BBC Radio's long-established, annual general knowledge competition for teams of secondary school children throughout the country. The teams are each made up of four members with ages ranging from eleven to eighteen. These schools have been the winners:

Top of the Form

1948	Royal High School, Edinburgh
1949	Elgin Academy, Scotland
1950	Robert Gordon's College, Aberdeen
1951	Morgan Academy, Dundee
1952	Bangor Grammar School, North Wales
1953	Nicholson Institute, Stornoway

1954	Grove Park School, Wrexham
1955	Newtown Girls' County Grammar School, Wales
1956	Sutton Coldfield High School
1957	Wycombe High School for Girls, High Wycombe
1958	Gordon Schools, Huntly, Aberdeenshire
1959	Mackie Academy, Stonehaven, Kincardine
1960	Grove Park Grammar School for Girls, Wrexham
1961	Archbishop Holgate's Grammar School, York
1962	Hull Grammar School
1963	Cambridgeshire High School for Boys, Cambridge
1964	The Academy, Montrose
1965	The High School, Falkirk
1966	St Martin-in-the-Fields High School, London
1967	Greenock Academy
1968	Grove Park School, Wrexham
1969	Queen Elizabeth Grammar School for Girls, Carmarthen
1970	Wyggeston Boys' School, Leicester
1971	Cheadle Hulme School, Cheadle, Cheshire
1972	The County Girls' Grammar School, Newbury
1973	Kirkcudbright Academy, Scotland
1974	The Grammar School, Cheltenham
1975	King William's College, Isle of Man
1976	County High School for Girls, Macclesfield
1977	Wellington School, Somerset
1978	Brinkburn School, Hartlepool
1979	Chislehurst & Sidcup Grammar School, Greater London.

University Challenge

Since 1964, Granada Television has organized the competition between teams from British universities. Here are the winners:

1964	Leicester University
1965	New College, Oxford
1966	Oriel College, Oxford

1967	University of Sussex
1968	Keble College, Oxford
1969	University of Sussex
1970	Churchill College, Cambridge
1971	Sidney Sussex College, Cambridge
1972	University College, Oxford
1973	Fitzwilliam College, Cambridge
1974	Trinity College, Cambridge
1975	Keble College, Oxford
1976	University College, Oxford
1977	University of Durham
1978	Sidney Sussex College, Cambridge
1979	*University Challenge* was not completed because of the ITV disruption.

RADIO

Top BBC Radio programmes in 1979

		Estimated audience
Radio 1:	*Top 40* (Sun)	c. $5\frac{1}{2}$ million
	Junior Choice (Sat)	c. $3\frac{1}{2}$ million
	Noel Edmonds (Sun)	c. 3 million
Radio 2:	Terry Wogan (weekdays)	peaks at 4 million
	Jimmy Young (weekdays)	c. $2\frac{1}{2}$ million
Radio 4:	8.00 a.m. *News*	c. 2 million
	8.10 a.m. *Today*	c. $1\frac{1}{2}$ million
	1.00 p.m. *News*	c. $1\frac{1}{2}$ million
	Any Questions (Sat)	c. 800 000
	Start the Week (Mon)	c. 700 000

Notable BBC Radio audiences

		estimated audience millions
Highest:	9 p.m. announcement of D-Day (6 June 1944)	25
Other large audiences	One talk in a series by Winston Churchill (average for series c. 19 million 1941/42)	24
	Christmas Day programme by Gracie Fields (1939)	23
	Have A Go (1948)	19½
	9.00 p.m. *News* during the war	16
	ITMA (end of 1944)	14½
	Henry Hall's *Guest Night* ⎤ during the	13
	Garrison Theatre ⎦ war	13
	Saturday Night Theatre (1944)	9
	Appointment with Fear (1944)	9
	Grand Hotel (1944)	9

Long-running BBC Radio programmes

Epilogue	began	26 September 1926
Any Questions	"	1 January 1941
From Our Own Correspondent	"	4 October 1946
Morning Service	"	14 January 1949
A Book at Bedtime	"	31 January 1949
The Archers	"	1 January 1951

RAILWAYS

The longest bridge isn't likely to get any longer, or the highest station to rise any more, at least not in the next few years, but the speed records will soon be increasing, thanks to the Advanced Passenger Train. The APT is electric, with the power car in the middle, and has a tilt mechanism which can take it round corners in safety and comfort at great speed – 40% faster than normal trains. It started on scheduled service in 1980.

The best of British Rail

Longest bridge: TAY BRIDGE 2 miles 365 yds

Bridge with longest span: FORTH BRIDGE two spans, each 1 710 ft

Highest railway bridge: BALLOCHMYLE VIADUCT (on the line between Glasgow and Carlisle) 164 ft above river bed

Longest tunnel: SEVERN TUNNEL 4 miles 628 yds

Longest straight: BETWEEN SELBY AND HULL 18 miles

Highest altitude: DRUIMUACHDAR 1 484 ft above sea level

Lowest point: SEVERN TUNNEL 144 ft below sea level

Steepest mainline gradient: LICKEY INCLINE 1 in 37·7 (nearly 2 miles)

Highest station: CORROUR, Invernessshire 1 327 ft

Station with most platforms: WATERLOO 21 platforms

Station with longest platform: COLCHESTER 1 920 ft

Busiest junction: CLAPHAM JUNCTION over 2 000 trains every weekday

Highest speeds: ADVANCED PASSENGER TRAIN 152 mph (3 August 1975) HIGH SPEED TRAIN 143 mph (12 June 1973)

Fastest scheduled passenger train: STEVENAGE-PETERBOROUGH, Inter-City 125 Average 106·25 mph

Fastest-ever train journey: PADDINGTON-CHIPPENHAM Inter-City 125 Average 111·7 mph (10 April 1979, possible world record)

Longest train journey: THE CLANSMAN – Euston-Inverness via Birmingham 568 miles

Heaviest train: carries iron ore, PORT TALBOT-LLANWERN 3 000 tonnes gross

Only BR steam route: VALE OF RHEIDOL LINE, Aberystwyth-Devil's Bridge 60 cm gauge: 11¾ miles

Number of trains every
twenty-four hours from London

	1978
Folkestone	35
Birmingham	31
Cardiff	25
Manchester	20
Norwich	19
Edinburgh	18
Hull	12
Glasgow	11
Aberdeen	9
Penzance	8
Inverness	5

READING

As befits a nation with the highest number of public libraries,
we head the European list for reading, though only just.

Percentage of people who
read books daily
in Europe 1974

Heron House

UK	21
Sweden Denmark }	20
W. Germany	18
Netherlands	15
Switzerland France }	14

Norway	⎫	13
Belgium	⎬	
Austria		12
Italy		9
Spain		7

RECORDS: GRAMOPHONE

We also do a lot of listening, at least we did in 1974 when this international survey was done. Record sales in the UK have fallen since then.

Total sales of gramophone
records per 1 000 inhabitants

Heron House estimates

	millions
UK	1 900
Canada	1 800
Australia	1 600
USA ⎫	
W. Germany ⎬	1 300
Sweden ⎭	
Belgium	1 100
France	1 000
Japan	800
Denmark	600
Norway ⎫	
Spain ⎬	500
Switzerland ⎭	
Austria	300
Italy	165

RECORDS: ODDEST

Roy Castle, who presents BBC TV's *The Record Breakers*, a show which is based on listings in the *Guinness Book of Records*, has chosen what he considers the oddest British ones he has come across so far. The comments after each record are Mr Castle's very own remarks . . .

1 *Camping out*
Graham Hurry, when a member of the 38th Coventry Central Scout Group, started sleeping outdoors on 19 June 1975 for a competition organized by *Scouting Magazine*. He carried on until 19 June 1978, having slept every night under canvas for four years.

'When he went back to the house his parents had moved.'

2 *Demolition*
On 4 June 1972, Phil Milner, who is a karate third dan, led fifteen members of the International Judo Association in the demolition of a six-roomed Victorian house at Idle, Bradford, using only their heads, feet and bare hands. It took them just six hours.

'Victorian cement takes years to dry. Don't use it.'

3 *Stair-climbing*
Bill Stevenson, a member of the Houses of Parliament Maintenance and Engineering Division, has had to climb 334 of the 364 steps of St Stephen's Tower 2 829 times in ten years. It is equivalent to climbing Mount Everest over seventeen times.

'Too mean to buy oxygen equipment – warm clothing . . . and a watch.'

4 *Fishing contest*
At Buckenham, Ferry, Norfolk, on 9 January 1977, Peter Christian took part in a fishing contest with 107 other competitors. He won by catching a fish that weighed one-sixteenth of an ounce.

'Ate it for tea – "off the bone".'

161

5 Football Bookings

On 3 November 1969, in a local cup match between Tongham Youth Club and Horley, the referee booked all twenty-two players and one of the linesmen. Tongham won 2–0, and the match was described by one of the players as 'a good, hard game'.

'The replay is at Wormwood Scrubs in three years. Two years with good conduct.'

In another football match at Waltham Abbey on 23 December 1973, M. J. Woodhams, refereeing a Gancia Cup match, sent off the entire Juventus-Cross team together with some of their officials.

'They lost 200 nil – all scored in the second half.'

6 Slow pigeon

On 29 September 1974, a pigeon named Blue Clip belonging to Harold Hart arrived home in its loft in Leigh, Greater Manchester. It had been released in Rennes, France over seven years earlier. The distance of 370 miles meant the pigeon had an average speed of 0·00589 mph which is slower than the world's fastest snail.

'It has also visited more unknown towns than any other pigeon.'

7 Singing

At a choral competition in Wales, only one choir entered, and did not even win the first prize. The judges said that as a punishment for arriving forty-five minutes late, they would only place them second.

'First prize was awarded to a tone-deaf busload who couldn't sing but arrived on time.'

8 Bus service

In 1976, it was reported that buses on the Hanley-Bagnoll route in Staffordshire would not stop for passengers. After complaints, Councillor Arthur Cholorton stated that if those buses stopped to pick up passengers, they would disrupt the timetable.

'Still applies. The service is in the red.'

9 *TV commercial*

Comedienne Pat Coombes had twenty-eight takes whilst making a commercial for a breakfast cereal. Each time she forgot the same thing – the name of the product. The commercial was never finished and the product was taken off the market.

'No one could remember it.'

10 *Animal rescue*

In 1978, during the firemen's strike, a lady in South London called in the Army to retrieve her cat which was trapped up a tree. They duly did so, but as they drove off, they ran over the cat and killed it.

'She was *afraid* to shout "HELP"! '

11 *Football Crowd*

On 7 May 1921, Leicester City played Stockport County at Manchester United's ground. Only thirteen people turned up to watch it.

'There was polo at Hurley.'

12 *Misprints*

On 22 August 1978, on page 19 of *The Times*, there were 97 misprints in $5\frac{1}{2}$ single column inches. The passage was about 'Pop' (Pope) Paul VI.

'It wsa mist unterusting reedink.'

RESTAURANTS

We asked Egon Ronay to list his personal favourites – British restaurants and hotels that he most enjoys visiting. This is his list and comments.

Egon Ronay's favourite
British restaurants and hotels

Les Ambassadeurs Club, Mayfair – 'For making me feel like a millionaire'
Le Gavroche, Chelsea – 'For its foie gras'

Gravetye Manor, Sussex – 'For their unparalleled cold buffet on Boxing Night'

Shezan, Knightsbridge – 'For letting gluttony get the better of me'

Tate Gallery Restaurant, Pimlico – 'To indulge regularly in some of the world's best wines at the price of third-rate ones'

Connaught, Mayfair – 'For the illusion that wealth prevails'

Inn on the Park, Mayfair – 'For its oiled wheels'

Inverlochy Castle, Scotland – 'For the feeling of staying at a grand country home'

Michael's Nook, Lake District – 'For impeccable service by its ex-amateur staff'

Sharrow Bay, Lake District – 'For the chintzy fussiness of its rooms'

RISKS OF DEATH

Activities that carry a million to one chance of death

Sir Edward Pochin of the National Radiological Protection Board

Smoking $1\frac{1}{2}$ cigarettes a day
Travelling 50 miles by car
Travelling 250 miles by air
Rock climbing for $1\frac{1}{2}$ minutes
Factory work for two weeks
Being a man aged sixty for 20 minutes

Chances of being killed per hour

Brian Silcock, The Sunday Times, December 1979

Professional boxing	1 in 14 000
Steeplechasing (per ride)	1 in 20 000
Rock climbing	1 in 25 000

Motor racing	1 in 30 000
Canoeing	1 in 100 000
Flat racing (per ride)	1 in 100 000
Skiing	1 in 1 150 000

Risks while travelling: chances of being killed per million miles

Brian Silcock, The Sunday Times, *December 1979*

Motor cycle	1 in 3
Horse	1 in 4
Bicycle	1 in 6
Car (driver)	1 in 66
Train	1 in 300
Aircraft	1 in 300
Bus passenger	1 in 500

ROLLS ROYCE

Yet again, another wonderful list where the UK leads the world.

Number of Rolls Royces bought in 1977

Rolls Royce

UK	1 450
USA	1 000
Middle East	173
New Caledonia	93
Ireland	82
France W. Germany }	70

Canada	64
Italy	55
Belgium	12
Denmark	1

ROMANCE

Barbara Cartland's ten most romantic men

1 Lord Mountbatten
2 The present Prince of Wales
3 Ronald Cartland (her brother)
4 Douglas Fairbanks Junior
5 Prince George, Duke of Kent
6 Fifth Duke of Sutherland
7 Noël Coward
8 Ivor Novello
9 Marquis of Bath
10 Jack Buchanan

Jan Kaluza asked Barbara Cartland for her reasons and got this reply: 'All the men on my list are glamorous and attractive with strong personalities and decisive characters. Of course all of them are or were frightfully good-looking, too – how can you possibly choose romantic men who aren't? I don't think there are many romantic, glamorous men around today. I was terribly disappointed when I went on a recent trip to Russia expecting to find a tall, dark and handsome prince, and all I saw were two-feet-tall pygmies.

'I've always preferred Englishmen. A lot of people say they aren't good lovers, but I think they're very sincere.

'There's so little romance about. Men take girls to bed without wooing them. It should be the last chapter, not the first.'

SALES

London is the world capital for sales of almost every sort. We asked the two leading auctioneers to compile some of their world-beating lists (see also under 'P' for Paintings).

Sotheby's sale records

The London-based firm of Sotheby Parke Barnet, the biggest fine-art auctioneers in the world, create world record prices almost every month. In the four months ending December 1979, the group had net sales of over £94 million, more than double that of any rival anywhere. This is how the money was broken down, department by department.

Departmental totals

Jewellery	£16 246 000
Impressionist, post-Impressionist and contemporary art	£12 091 000
18th-19th- and 20th-Century British and Continental paintings and drawings	£10 626 000
Furniture	£7 966 000
Works of art (including sculpture, musical instruments, arms and armour)	£8 309 000
Silver	£5 431 000
Chinese	£4 723 000
Old Master paintings and drawings	£4 413 000
North American and South African works of art	£3 875 000
Books and manuscripts	£2 952 000
Postage stamps	£2 634 000
Prints	£2 576 000
European ceramics and glass	£2 524 000
Rugs and carpets	£2 423 000
Clocks and watches	£2 129 000
Antiquities	£1 749 000
Japanese works of art	£1 160 000

Art Nouveau	£875 000
Photographs and allied materials	£600 000
Wine	£552 000
Coins and medals	£481 000
	£94 335 000

The Jewellery Department was helped into its lead by a sale Sotheby held in Zurich on 7 November 1979 when £770 000 was paid for an emerald and diamond tiara – a world auction record for any single piece of jewellery.

Sotheby's assorted world records, 1979

1 *World record for Japanese ivory figure*
Gashinsai Meigyoku ivory group of Kokaku and his
mother, *c.* 1870 .... £6 400

2 *World record for Woodall cameo glass*
Vase entitled 'Undine' – signed Geo. Woodall,
c. 1885 .... £19 000

3 *World record for a Chiparus figure*
A large Chiparus bronze and ivory group of a
dancing couple, 1920s £6 200

4 *World record for a typewriter*
A Velograph typewriter, Swiss, *c.* 1887 .... £1 100

5 *World record for an Assyrian antiquity*
Relief depicting a winged human-headed deity
or genie, *c.* 883–859 BC £240 000

6 *World record for a Russian icon*
Double-sided processional icon (48·5 × 38 cm),
Novgorod 1531 .... £25 000

7 *World record for English furniture*
George III ormolu-mounted commode, attributed
to Pierre Langlois, 2ft 9in high by 5ft 1in
wide by 2ft 1½in deep, *c.* 1760 .... £120 000

8 *World record for a medical book*
De Motu Cordis, first edition, Frankfurt, 1628,
by William Harvey. One of 57 copies known £88 000
9 *World record for an automaton*
A rare musical 'singing bird' automaton, 70 cm high,
the movement signed 'Richard, Rue des
Prouvaires à Paris' and dated 1757 £106 741
10 *World record for farm accounts*
Ely Abbey's 11th-Century Farm Accounts £52 000
11 *Pirelli Calendar, 1973*
Bought by the Tate Gallery (February 1980) £44

Christie's assorted
world records

Jewellery
1 Highest total for a jewellery sale anywhere
in the world – London, 22 November 1979 £6 785 085
2 Emerald and diamond ring of 12·64 cts –
record price of $48 240 per carat £285 714
3 Ruby and diamond ring of 4·12 cts –
record price of $100 639 per carat £194 285
4 Sapphire and diamond ring of 11·81 cts –
record price of $25 815 per carat £142 857
5 Record auction price for a single 'lot'
of diamonds – a pair of drop-shaped diamonds of
42·50 and 44·93 cts £640 000
Books
Gutenberg Bible – record auction price for a
printed book £1 176 000
Silver
Pair of Louis XV soup tureens by Juste-Aurele
Meissonier – record auction price for a single
lot of silver £612 500
17th-century ewer by Adam van Vianen – record
auction price for a single piece of silver £164 686

Drawings
The Newall Collection of English Drawings
and Watercolours – highest total for a sale of
English drawings and watercolours £782 885
Art Nouveau and Art Deco
Galle marqueterie de verre cup – record auction
price for a piece of Art Nouveau £104 815
Tiffany spider-web leaded-glass, mosaic and
bronze table lamp – record auction price for a
piece of Tiffany glass £75 000
Lalique choker – record auction price for a work by
Lalique £48 295
Art Nouveau marquetry *meuble à deux corps* by
Emile Galle £22 857
Works of Art
White marble bust of Mon. Antonio Cerri by
Alessandro Algardi – record auction price for a
classical sculpture £150 000
Clocks and watches
Bracket clock by Thomas Tompion – record
auction price for an English clock £65 000
Cars
Mercedes-Benz roadster of 1936 – record
auction price for any car £210 520
Icons
Presentation of The Virgin Mary in the Temple –
record auction price for any icon £36 764
Wine
1806 Château-Lafite – record auction price for a
single bottle £8 300
1822 Château-Lafite £3 500 per bottle
1961 Château Petrus – record auction price
for a post-war vintage £500 per 3 bottles
Russian works of art
Nicholas II equestrian egg by Carl Fabergé –
record auction price for a work by Fabergé £125 000
Camera
Stereoscopic camera by J. B. Dancer, 1856 –
record auction price for any camera £21 000
170

Glass
Elizabethan dated presentation glass –
record auction price for an English glass   £75 000
St Louis gingham pattern upright bouquet
weight – record auction price for a paperweight   £48 000

SCHOOLS

During the 1978-9 academic year, these are the schools which got the most open awards – scholarships and exhibitions – to Oxford and Cambridge. It was considered a fairly typical year, except for the rise in the number of girls getting awards to Oxford, 251, compared with 146 the previous year. At Cambridge, girls got 166 awards, compared with 168 the year before. Girls' schools have been underlined in the list.

No account has been taken of the fact that some schools are private and some State-aided, nor of the differing sizes of schools. Manchester Grammar School and Eton, for example, are double the size of the average school on this list.

Top schools: Oxbridge awards

Manchester Grammar School	33
Eton College	28
St Paul's	26
Dulwich College	25
Bradford Grammar School	23
Westminster	21
Winchester College	20
Haberdashers Aske's, Elstree	18
Latymer Upper	17
Nottingham High School	16
Newcastle Royal Grammar School	15

Brentwood	14
City of London	14
Oundle	14
Rugby	14
King's College School, Wimbledon	13
King's School, Canterbury	13
Perse School for Girls, Cambridge	13
Sherborne	13
Whitgift School, Croydon	13
Birkenhead	12
Charterhouse	12
King Edward's School, Birmingham	12
Marlborough College	12
Bradford Girls' Grammar School	11
Bristol Grammar School	11
Merchant Taylors', Northwood	11
St Paul's Girls' School	11
Sevenoaks	11
Shrewsbury	11
Solihull	11
Uppingham	11
Lancing College	10
St Alban's	10
Aylesbury Grammar School	9
Coventry	9
High Wycombe Royal Grammar School	9
Queen Elizabeth Grammar School, Blackburn	9
Trinity School, Croydon	9
Bedford	8
Bury Grammar School	8
Clifton College	8
Epsom College	8
George Watson's College, Edinburgh	8
William Ellis	8
Wolverhampton Grammar School	8
Ampleforth College	7
Cheltenham Ladies' College	7
Chislehurst and Sidcup Grammar School	7

Christ's Hospital	7
Cranleigh	7
Harrogate Grammar School	7
Harrow	7
King's School, Worcester	7
Leeds Grammar School	7
Malvern College	7
Millfield	7
Perse School for Boys', Cambridge	7
Wellington College	7
Bolton (Boys' Division)	6
Camden School for Girls	6
Dr Challoner's Grammar School, Amersham	6
Edinburgh Academy	6
Eltham College	6
Glenalmond (Trinity College)	6
Haileybury College	6
North London Collegiate	6
Radley College	6
St Leonard's Mayfield	6
Stowe	6

Some famous
early school-leavers

People with a minimal basic education who left school at an early age but who succeeded in their respective professions:

George Stephenson – father of the railways
Charlie Chaplin – actor
Adolf Hitler – German dictator
Andrew Carnegie – philanthropist
Noël Coward – playwright
Charles Dickens – novelist

SCIENTISTS

Sir Peter Medawar, the Nobel Prize winner, has compiled this list of the men he considers to be the greatest British scientists of all time. All of them, in his opinion, are giant figures.

Britain's greatest
scientists and thinkers

1 **Francis Bacon**: 1561–1626   English philosopher and statesman: 'He was the first great methodological scientist in history.'

2 **Thomas Hobbes**: 1588–1679   English philosopher, author of *Leviathan*: 'He was the first great materialist philosopher.'

3 **David Hume**: 1711–76   Scottish philosopher: 'The foremost philosopher of the mind.'

4 **Michael Faraday**: 1791–1867   English physicist, discovered electro-magnetism. 'He was the greatest experimentalist that has ever been. A marvellous man.'

5 **William Whewell**: 1794–1866   English philosopher and historian. Master of Trinity College, Cambridge. 'He was a polymath who amongst many things invented the word scientist.'

6 **Charles Darwin**: 1809–82   English naturalist, author of *The Origin of Species*: 'Darwin wears very well. His greatness becomes increasingly evident as one re-studies his writings, which is something one can't say about many people.'

7 **Bertrand Russell**: 1872–1970   English philosopher: 'The foremost mathematician philosopher of his day.'

8 **Karl Popper**: born Vienna 1902 British citizen, philosopher. 'He's the principal philosopher of science in the world today.'

9 **Sir Ernst Gombrich**: born Vienna 1909 British citizen, historian of culture: 'The wisest and most learned man I have ever known.'

SEEDS

Ten top-selling individual
varieties of vegetable seeds
Suttons Seeds

Each vegetable comes in many varieties, some more popular
than others. Even though lettuces as a whole are the most
popular of all vegetables, it is an individual variety of beetroot
which sells best of all the different seed packets.

1 Beetglobe (beetroot)
2 White Lisbon (onion)
3 Champion Scarlet Horn (carrot)
4 Tender and True (parsnip)
5 Webb's Wonderful (lettuce)
6 Imperial Curled (parsley)
7 Crimson French Breakfast (radish)
8 Beetboltardy (beetroot)
9 Curled (cress)
10 Suzen (lettuce)

Five top-selling pea and
bean seeds
Suttons Seeds

1 Onward (pea)
2 Enorma (runner bean)
3 The Prince (dwarf bean)
4 Scarlet Emperor (runner bean)
5 Kelvedon Wonder (pea)

Ten top-selling varieties
of flower seeds

Suttons Seeds

1 Nasturtium
2 Wallflower, Persian Carpet
3 Wallflower, Choice Mixed
4 Sweet pea, Suttons' Special Mixture
5 Lobelia, Crystal Palace
6 Candytuft, Dwarf Fairy Mixed
7 Pansy, Giant Fancy Mixed
8 Nemesia, Carnival Mixed
9 Nasturtium, Tall Single Mixed
10 Stock, Brompton Mixed

120–230 million seed packets – vegetables, peas and beans and flowers – are sold in the UK every year. In 1978, 34% of all UK gardens grew vegetables and 27% grew flowers. The total seed value is approximately £22 million per year. Seedsmen do best in times of economic gloom. The longer the dole queue, the more the vegetables are grown in the garden.

SEX

Most-used contraceptives

The Family Planning Association keep yearly figures of women (and men) using birth control methods. The figures for 1978 were:

	contraceptive	number of users
1	The Pill	3 100 000
2	The sheath	2 700 000
3	Coitus interruptus	700 000
4	Sterilization	600 000

5 IUD	600 000
6 Diaphragm	300 000
7 Rhythm method	200 000
8 Injectables, i.e. Depo-Provera	33 000

There are in Great Britain approximately 11 million women in the fertile age range 15–44. Of these, 8 million are likely to be sexually active, and of these 8 million, 3 million women or their partners are thought not to be using any reliable form of contraception, or are irregular users.

The Pill remains the leader – although figures have dropped in recent years. In 1976, 3·6 million women were taking the Pill and in 1977 3·5 million. It is expected to settle down to around the 3 million mark for some years. Could birth control by injection be the thing of the 80s? The Family Planning Association think not. 'It is only recommended for limited use,' says a FPA spokesman, 'such as when a husband has had a vasectomy, or a girl has had a German measles injection and it would be dangerous for her to get pregnant in the following three months. It is a hormonal contraceptive and doesn't suit everyone.'

SEX SHOPS

We sent an intrepid investigator, in an old raincoat, to Ann Summers Ltd, 16 Tottenham Court Road, London, W1, to ask what was selling well:

Sex-shop best-sellers

1 Magazines: *Rustler, Rapier, Journal of Sex*, price £1·20
2 Books: *Sexual Knowledge*, £6·00; *Sex In and Out of Marriage*, £2·50; *How to Improve Your Man in Bed*, £1.
3 Vibrators: 'Humming Bird de Luxe', £4·00; 'Stallion Vibrator', £6·90.

4 Films (blue movies): *A Tramp in Paradise*, 200 ft Super & Colour; silent £20, sound £32·50; *Go Down, My Love*, silent £23, Sound £33.
5 Sexual stimulants: 'Action spray – for a proud man!', 'Taurus love-life tablets', £3·50 each.
6 Sex Maniac's Diary, £2·50.
7 Underwear (kinky): wet look; satin; see-through nylon for both sexes, £1·50 – £4 for small items; £7·50 – £25 for nighties.
8 Rubber wear: cat suits, bras, masks, spanking trousers, raincoats, £7·95 – £68·50.
9 Dolls: 'Living Doll', 'Miss Wonderful', £14·80 – £180.
10 Video tapes VHS: *Hot vibrations*, £39·95, 20 minutes each side.

SHAKESPEARE

Trevor Nunn, director of the Royal Shakespeare Company, has arranged the complete Shakespeare canon in order of his personal favourites. His first choice might surprise many people.

1 *The Winter's Tale*
2 *Twelfth Night*
3 *Henry IV Part 2*
4 *King Lear*
5 *The Tempest*
6 *Hamlet*
7 *As You Like It*
8 *Much Ado About Nothing*
9 *A Midsummer Night's Dream*
10 *All's Well That Ends Well*
11 *Henry IV Part 1*
12 *Henry V*
13 *Troilus and Cressida*
14 *Coriolanus*

15 *Julius Caesar*
16 *Macbeth*
17 *Othello*
18 *Antony and Cleopatra*
19 *Cymbeline*
20 *Timon of Athens*
21 *Measure for Measure*
22 *The Comedy of Errors*
23 *The Merry Wives of Windsor*
24 *Love's Labours Lost*
25 *Romeo and Juliet*
26 *The Taming of the Shrew*
27 *The Merchant of Venice*
28 *Two Gentlemen of Verona*
29 *Pericles*
30 *Richard III*
31 *Richard II*
32 *Henry VI Part 3*
33 *Henry VI Part 2*
34 *Henry VI Part 1*
35 *King John*
36 *Titus Andronicus*
37 *Henry VIII*

SHERRIES

And now for a list in very good taste . . .

Top sherries sold in the UK

1 Harvey's Bristol Cream
2 Croft Original
3 Harvey's Club Amontillado
4 Double Century Oloroso (Domecq)
5 Double Century Cream (Domecq)

Sherry is the most popular alcoholic drink in the UK, apart from beer, and is drunk by the widest range of people. The total sherry market of 1979 was an estimated 6 million cases – ranging from Harvey's Bristol Cream to Sainsbury's own brand.

The sherry taste preference in Britain is predominantly sweet (sweet 57%, medium 30%, dry 13%) though there is a slight but growing trend to preferring a drier sherry.

SONGS

An annual competition is held for BBC television viewers to vote for Britain's entry in the Eurovision Song Contest. An asterisk signifies the entries which subsequently won the European title.

Britain's songs for Europe

1957 'All', Patricia Bredin
1958 No entry
1959 'Sing Little Birdie', Teddy Johnson and Pearl Carr
1960 'Looking High, High, High', Bryan Johnson
1961 'Are You Sure?', The Allisons
1962 'Ring-A-Ding Girl', Ronnie Carroll
1963 'Say Wonderful Things', Ronnie Carroll
1964 'I Love the Little Things', Matt Monro
1965 'I Belong', Kathy Kirby
1966 'A Man Without Love', Kenneth McKellar
1967 'Puppet on a String', Sandie Shaw★
1968 'Congratulations', Cliff Richard
1969 'Boom-Bang-a-Bang', Lulu
1970 'Knock, Knock, Who's There?', Mary Hopkins
1971 'Jack in the Box', Clodagh Rodgers
1972 'Beg, Steal or Borrow', The New Seekers
1973 'Power to All Our Friends', Cliff Richard
1974 'Long Live Love', Olivia Newton-John

1975	'Let Me Be The One', The Shadows
1976	'Save Your Kisses for Me', Brotherhood of Man*
1977	'Rock Bottom', Lynsey de Paul and Mike Moran
1978	'The Bad Old Days', Co-Co
1979	'Mary Ann', Black Lace

SPORT

Most of our sports lists are under individual headings, such as C for Cricket, F for Football, but here is a general sports list.

The BBC sports personality of the Year

Each year viewers of *Grandstand* and other BBC television sports programmes cast their votes to find the year's outstanding sports personality. These are the winners since the competition began:

1954	Christopher Chataway (athletics)
1955	Gordon Pirie (athletics)
1956	Jim Laker (cricket)
1957	Dai Rees (golf)
1958	Ian Black (swimming)
1959	John Surtees (motor cycling)
1960	David Broome (show jumping)
1961	Stirling Moss (motor racing)
1962	Anita Lonsborough (swimming)
1963	Dorothy Hyman (athletics)
1964	Mary Rand (athletics)
1965	Tommy Simpson (cycling)
1966	Bobby Moore (football)
1967	Henry Cooper (boxing)
1968	David Hemery (athletics)

1969 Ann Jones (tennis)
1970 Henry Cooper (boxing)
1971 Princess Anne (show jumping)
1972 Mary Peters (athletics)
1973 Jackie Stewart (motor racing)
1974 Brendan Foster (athletics)
1975 David Steele (cricket)
1976 John Curry (ice skating)
1977 Virginia Wade (tennis)
1978 Steve Ovett (athletics)
1979 Sebastian Coe (athletics)

STAMPS

Stamp collecting is the world's most popular collecting hobby. (Of all the world's hobbies, it is generally ranked as number two after photography.) There are two million serious stamp collectors in Britain.

As investments, few things have increased more dramatically in price in the last decade. On average, classic stamps (pre-1900) have increased by 15–25 per cent a year. Many have gone up five times in value in the last five years.

These 1980 lists have been provided by Stanley Gibbons, London, the largest international stamp dealers in the world. During 1979 they created a world record for a single stamp collection when they paid (US) $10 million, £5 million, for the Marc Hass collection of early United States' postal covers.

The top ten British stamps
(approximate values, 1980)

1 1902–4 King Edward VII 6d, dull
   purple, Inland Revenue overprint   £45 000 unused
                                           £25 000 used

2 1882 Queen Victoria £1, brown-lilac,
(watermark large anchor)   £28 000 unused
                                          £1 900 used
3 1864–79 Queen Victoria 1d, red, plate 77   £27 000 unused
                                          £16 000 used
4 1878 Queen Victoria £1, brown-lilac,
(watermark Maltese cross)   £25 000 unused
                                          £1 200 used
5 1902–4 King Edward VII 1/-, green and
red, Board of Education overprint   £22 000 unused
                                          £10 000 used
6 1883 Queen Victoria 10/-, grey
(watermark large anchor)   £20 000 unused
                                          £1 000 used
7 1878 Queen Victoria 10/-, grey
(watermark Maltese Cross)   £19 000 unused
                                          £850 used

1888 Queen Victoria £1, brown-lilac,
Inland Revenue overprint (watermark
three crowns)   £19 000 unused
                                          £1 300 used
8 1890 Queen Victoria £1, brown-lilac,
Inland Revenue overprint (watermark
three crowns)   £17 000 unused
                                          £2 750 used
9 1902 King Edward VII 10/-, blue,
Inland Revenue overprint   £16 000 unused
                                          £9 000 used
10 1890 Queen Victoria £1, brown-lilac,
Inland Revenue overprint (watermark
three orbs)   £14 000 unused
                                          £2 500 used

1902 King Edward VII £1, green,
Inland Revenue overprint   £14 000 unused
                                          £3 000 used

Notice that a Penny Black, Britain's best-known stamp, is
not in the list. Although it was the first postage stamp in the
world in 1840, 69 million were printed. However, according

to the 1980 S. G. catalogue, a Penny Black in good condition is worth around £2 000, and a Tuppenny Blue £4 500.

The top ten world stamps
(approximate values, 1980)

1	British Guiana 1 cent, black on magenta of 1856	£425 000 unused
2	Mauritius 'Post Office' penny red of 1847	£300 000 unused
		£110 000 used
3	Mauritius 'Post Office' tuppenny blue of 1847	£190 000 unused
		£110 000 used
4	Bermuda red 'Penny Perot' 1848–61	£100 000 used
5	Hawaii 2 cents blue of 1851	£60 000 unused
		£30 000 used
6	British Guiana 2 cents rose 'Cotton Reel' 1851	£45 000 used
7	Great Britain 1902 sixpenny purple, Inland Revenue overprint	£45 000 unused
		£25 000 used
8	Ceylon fourpenny dull rose of 1857	£40 000 unused
		£3 000 used
9	Canada 12d black of 1851	£33 000 unused
		£30 000 used
10	Great Britain, 1882 Queen Victoria £1	£28 000 unused

The top ten prices realized

Prices paid at Stanley Gibbons public auctions in London during the 1970s.

1	British Guiana 'Miss Rose' cover	£70 000
2	1851 12d on laid paper	£51 000
3	Bermuda 1848–56 penny 'Perot' on cover	£50 000
4	Mauritius 1841 penny 'Post Office'	£50 000

5 Cape of Good Hope 1861 'Woodblock'
  fourpenny, error of colour £45 000
6 1851 New Carlisle 'Gaspe' colour £31 000
7 Bermuda 1848–56 penny 'Perot' £30 000
8 Saxony 1850 3pf. block of six £28 000
9 British Guiana 1850–51 4c., 8c. on cover £25 000
10 New Brunswick 1851 1/- bisect cover £21 000

STOCKS AND BONDS

The top ten old bonds, 1980

Stanley Gibbons also deal in old bonds and share certificates, a
new hobby which began in Germany in 1973 and started
seriously in Britain in 1977. Old shares, many from bankrupt or
long dead companies, and formerly considered worthless,
immediately started changing hands at huge prices.

1 Chinese 1898 4½% Gold Loan, un-issued stock,
  from the Deutsch-Asiatische Bank:
  denomination £500 £15 000
  denomination £50 (reported 45 in existence) £5 000
  denomination £25 (reported 45 in existence) £5 000
2 Chinese 1903 5% Emprunt Chinois,
  denomination 500 francs type II, un-issued
  reserve stock (4 in existence) £7 500
3 Chinese 1903 5% Emprunt Chinois,
  denomination 500 francs type 1, un-issued reserve
  stock (8 in existence) £7 500
4 Chinese 1912 6% treasury bill, denomination
  1000 Shanghai taels   type D £7 500
                            type E £7 500
                            type C £6 500
                            type B £5 500

5 Chinese 1913 Austrian Loan 6% denomination
£1000	£5 000
denomination £500	£3 500

 6 Chinese 1918 8% Marconi treasury bill
denomination £1 000	£5 000
denomination £500 (with original coupons)	£4 000

 7 Russian 1909 City of Nicholaiev 500 roubles
denomination 1500	£4 500

 8 Chinese 1919 8% Vickers treasury notes
denomination £500 (with original coupons)	£4 000
denomination £1000	£3 500

 9 Russian 1822 5% Rothschild loan £1 036 bond,
type A	£3 500

10 German 1927 City of Dresden 5½% sterling loan;
denomination £1 000	£3 500

SUICIDE

Suicides per 100,000 inhabitants, 1974

World Health Organization

Denmark	26
Austria	24
W. Germany / Switzerland	20
Sweden	19
Japan	17
Belgium / France	15
Canada	13
USA	12
Australia	11

Netherlands		
Norway	}	10
UK		8
Italy		5
Spain		4
Ireland		3

It must be all that reading which helps Britons to take their minds off their troubles, or watching all those Rolls Royces, or reading about the phenomenal prices paid at London auction houses . . . Incidentally, notice that Sweden is not number one, despite all the nasty rumours.

SURNAMES

The most common surnames
in England and Wales

This is a traditional list, reproduced in several books, but accepted by most people as fairly accurate. Complete accuracy would be difficult to achieve, with almost 50 million names to count . . .

1 Smith
2 Jones
3 Williams
4 Brown
5 Taylor
6 Davies
7 Evans
8 Thomas
9 Roberts
10 Johnson

It is noticeable how common Welsh names are in this total list – Jones, Williams, Davies, Evans and Roberts – when

Wales is by far the smaller of the two nations, with a population of under 3m, compared with England's 46m. They've obviously moved into England, and bred fast.

The most common surnames in the London telephone directory

As a check on the previous list, we counted their individual listings in the London Telephone Directory. Where the same firm, such as W. H. Smith, had many phone numbers, we counted it as only one. The object was to try to count *different* people or firms with the same surname. These are the top ten, to the nearest 100, different listings.

1	Smith	9 500
2	Jones	5 000
3	Brown	4 300
4	Williams	4 000
5	Taylor	3 600
6	Davis	2 500
7	Johnson	2 500
8	Thomas	2 300
9	Davies	2 200
10	Evans	2 200

Smith triumphed once again, covering twenty-five pages, double the nearest rival, and again the Welsh were to the fore, though Roberts in London is replaced by the anglicized Davis. If Davis and Davies were added together, which of course would not be acceptable to the Davies clan, being of superior pedigree, their total would be 4 700 and put them into third position in London.

SYMPHONIES

Analysis of all the symphonies scheduled for performance in London during 1979 – at the Royal Albert Hall, the Festival Halls on the South Bank and St John's, Smith Square – showed that Beethoven was the composer performed most often for the 28th consecutive year.

The most popular composers of symphonies

letter in The Times *from David Chesterman,*
(3 January 1980)

1	Beethoven	42
2	Mozart	34
3	Haydn	26
4	Mahler	22
5	Brahms	21
6	Tchaikovsky	19
7	Dvorak	16
8	Schubert and Shostakovitch	15
9	Sibelius	11
10	Bruckner	10

Haydn made the biggest leap, from eighth to third place. Predictions for 1980 were that Mahler and Shostakovitch would both rise.

TELEPHONE CALLS

Total calls in 1970–71 for the eight services listed below were 366 million. By 1978–9, the figure had risen to 598 million. Overall, telephone usage per head has increased by about six per cent a year over the past thirty years. The number of ex-directory telephone numbers is also increasing, and some 856 thousand numbers were not in the directories in February 1979.

Calls to information services

Telecommunications Statistics Post Office

		year in which service came into operation	millions of calls
1	Speaking clock	1936	431·2
2	Dial a disc	1966	110·3
3	Weather	1956	29·0
4	Cricket	1956	18·0
5	*Financial Times* index	1969	4·0
6	Motoring	1956	2·7
7	Dial a recipe	1961	2·3
8	Teletourist	1958	0·6

TELEPHONES

Telephones in use per 1 000 population

1	USA	677
2	Denmark	428
3	Luxembourg	397
4	UK	366
5	Japan	356
6	Netherlands	344
7	W. Germany	302
8	Belgium	272
9	Italy	246
10	France	236
11	Irish Republic	127
12	USSR	62

TELEVISION

Television receivers in use per 1 000 population

EEC statistics, 1975

1	USA	571
2	UK	315
3	Denmark	308
4	W. Germany	305
5	Netherlands	259
6	Luxembourg	257
7	Belgium	252
8	France	235
9	Japan	233
10	Italy	213
11	USSR	208
12	Irish Republic	178

Top TV advertisers, 1979

Jictar/Tempo/ITCA

Advertiser	Expenditure
1 Proctor & Gamble Ltd (washing powders, soaps, etc)	10 325 468
2 Mars Ltd (confectionery)	7 852 811
3 Rowntree Mackintosh Ltd (confectionery)	6 761 975
4 Cadbury Ltd (confectionery)	6 288 833
5 Central Office of Information (anti-smoking, anti-drinking and driving, Keep Britain Tidy campaigns, etc)	6 047 737
6 United Biscuits Ltd	5 719 048
7 Beecham Products (medicines, shampoos)	5 482 931
8 Lever Bros (washing powders, washing-up liquids, etc)	5 433 496
9 Pedigree Petfoods (dog and cat foods)	5 139 799

191

10	Van Den Berghs (margarine, cooking fats)	5 066 747
11	Elida Gibbs Ltd (shampoos, toothpastes, cosmetic creams, etc)	4 578 138
12	General Foods Ltd (custards, instant coffee, etc)	4 433 056
13	H. J. Heinz & Co Ltd	4 415 179
14	Philips Electrical Ltd (TVs, hi-fis, etc)	4 040 332
15	Birds Eye Foods Ltd	3 794 095
16	Post Office (Busby, etc)	3 473 695
17	Brooke Bond Oxo Co	3 425 922
18	Milk Marketing Board	3 337 709
19	Reckitt & Colman (medicines, foods, honey)	3 275 867
20	F. W. Woolworth & Co	3 268 392

Top TV programmes, 1979

Jictar

In terms of the number of viewers, these were the most popular programmes during 1979, on either BBC or ITV. Where a programme is part of a series, the figure represents the episode which had the highest viewers during the year.

The figure in brackets is the number of times the series appeared in the Top Five Charts issued monthly during the year by JICTAR. During the year an industrial dispute took ITV off the air for several weeks, but even so, BBC had by far the most popular programmes.

			millions
1	*To The Manor Born* (3)	BBC 1	24·00
2	Larry Grayson's *Generation Game* (4)	BBC 1	23·85
3	*Blankety Blank* (5)	BBC 1	23·30
4	*Are You Being Served?* (1)	BBC 1	22·60
5	*Mastermind* (1)	BBC 1	22·55
6	Mike Yarwood *In Persons* (1)	BBC 1	21·10
7	*Secret Army* (1)	BBC 1	20·95
8	*The Last of the Summer Wine* (1)	BBC 1	20·90
9	*The Benny Hill Show* (3)	Thames	20·85

10	*Shoestring* (1)	BBC 1	19·90
11	*Coronation Street* (13)	Granada	19·50
12	*The Poseidon Adventure* (1)	BBC 1	
	It's a Celebrity Knockout (1)	BBC 1	19·30
	This Is Your Life (4)	Thames	
13	*Juggernaut* (1)	BBC 1	19·25
14	*Dirty Money* (1)	ITV	19·10
15	*Nine O'Clock News* (1)	BBC 1	18·95
16	*Miss United Kingdom 1979* (1)	BBC 1	
	The Two Ronnies (2)	BBC 1	18·40
17	*Seaside Special* (1)	BBC 1	17·90
18	*The Great Escape* (1)	BBC 1	17·75
19	*Where Eagles Dare* (1)	BBC 1	17·50
20	*Porridge* (1)	BBC 1	
	Mid-Week Sports Special (2)	ITV	17·45
21	*It'll Be Alright On The Night* (1)	LWT	17·15
22	*Starsky and Hutch* (1)	BBC 1	17·05
23	*The TV Times Awards* (1)	Thames	16·75
24	*The Dick Emery Comedy Hour* (1)	Thames	15·50
25	*Crossroads* (1)	ATV	15·15
26	*In Loving Memory* (1)	Yorkshire	14·85
27	*Explorers of the Deep* (1)	BBC 1	13·40
28	*Ask The Family* (1)	BBC 1	13·35

All time top BBC
TV programmes

	year	estimated audience millions
Royal Variety Performance	1965	30
"	1962	30
"	1964	28·5
Morecambe and Wise Christmas Show	1977	28·5
World Cup Final: England v. W. Germany	1966	28
To the Manor Born	1979	27·5

Morecambe and Wise Christmas Show	1975	27·5
Miss World	1968	27·5
World Cup Semi-Final: England v. Portugal	1966	27·5
Steptoe and Son	1964	27·5
World Heavyweight Championship: Joe Frazier v. Cassius Clay	1971	27
Miss World	1969	27
Steptoe and Son	1964	27
Morecambe and Wise Christmas Show	1976	27
Larry Grayson's *Generation Game*	1979	27
Miss World	1970	26·5
Miss World	1967	26·5
Steptoe and Son	1964	26·5
Sound of Music (film)	1978	26·5
The Poseidon Adventure (film)	1979	26·5
Miss World	1971	26
World Cup: England v. W. Germany	1970	26
Apollo 13 Splashdown	1970	26
European Cup Final: Man. United v. Benfica	1968	26
Apollo 8 Splashdown	1968	26
Mike Yarwood Christmas Show	1977	26

NOTE: These are official BBC figures. It will be noticed that JICTAR, the independent body which also measures audience figures, gives a lower figure for *To the Manor Born* in the previous list.

Top types of BBC
TV programmes

		estimated audience millions
best watched films:	*The Sound of Music* (Christmas, 1978)	$26\frac{1}{2}$
	The Poseidon Adventure (Week 31, 1979)	
sports programme:	World Cup Final: England v. W. Germany (1966)	28

crime series:	*Starsky and Hutch* (1966)	av. 17
drama series:	*Colditz* (1972)	av. 16½
situation comedy programme:	*Steptoe and Son* (1964)	av. 26½
documentary:	*The Royal Family* (1969)	23
light entertainment series:	*Generation Game* (1979)	27

Long-running BBC TV programmes

Come Dancing	29 September 1950
The Good Old Days	20 July 1953
Panorama	11 November 1953
Sportsnight (originally *Sportsview*)	8 April 1954
TV News	5 July 1954
Crackerjack	14 September 1955
Grandstand	11 October 1958
Blue Peter	16 October 1958
The Sky at Night	20 October 1963
Top of the Pops	1 January 1964
Horizon	2 May 1964
Match of the Day	22 August 1964
Ask the Family	12 July 1967
Nationwide	9 September 1969
Play for Today	15 October 1970

Long-running ITV programmes

These are currently the longest running networked series from the ITV stations, with their dates of birth.

1 *What the Papers Say* (Granada)	5 November 1956
2 *Coronation Street* (Granada)	9 December 1960

3 *Survival* (Anglia)   1 February 1961
4 *University Challenge* (Granada)   21 September 1962
5 *Crossroads* (ATV)   2 November 1964

About Anglia is the longest running local news magazine on any ITV station (Anglia). – 2 June 1960

Terry Wogan's worst
TV programmes

Terry Wogan, the well-known *Blankety Blank* person, has included in his list of worst TV programmes some that he can't stand watching personally, such as his number one choice, and some he loves watching because they are so awful, such as his number three and four choices. 'I love to hate really cheap American programmes where they sit by the pool in a force ten gale and the wind blows their coiffeur all over the place.' His dislike of Marx Brothers films is genuine. 'I find them so unfunny, especially Harpo.' So is his dislike of horses, wrestlers and the 'arts', when it has inverted commas round it.

 1 *Blankety Blank*
 2 *Beggar Man, Thief*
 3 *Dallas*
 4 *Petrocelli*
 5 Anything to do with horses
 6 Anything to do with wrestling
 7 Any old Marx Brothers' movies
 8 Any 'Arts' programmes
 9 *Charlie's Angels*
10 *The Sword of Justice*
11 *The Time Express*

TENNIS

Britain's top tennis
players, 1980

This is the ranking list announced by the Lawn Tennis Association for 1980. The figure in brackets is the 1979 ranking. Virginia Wade was the number one woman for the ninth successive year.

Men
1 C. J. Mottram (Surrey) (1)
2 M. Cox (Leics) (3)
3 J. A. Lloyd (Essex) (2)
4 R. A. Lewis (Middx) (8)
5 J. Feaver (Dorset) (6)
6 R. Drysdale (Essex) (4)
7 A. Jarrett (Derbys) (5)
8 J. R. Smith (Devon) (7)
9 D. A. Lloyd (Essex) (10)
10 C. Bradnam (Middx) (15)
11 J. Whiteford (Sussex) (17)
12 R. Beven (Sussex) (11)
13 W. Davies (Lancs) (14)
14 M. Appleton (Lancs) (16)
15 J. Dier (Sussex) (18)
16 R. Booth (Hants) (–)
17 N. Sears (Sussex) (–)
18 H. Becker (Middx) (–)
19 K. Harris (Essex) (–)
20 N. Rayner (Essex) (19)

Women
1 S. V. Wade (Kent) (1)
2 S. Barker (Devon) (2)
3 A. Hobbs (Ches) (4)
4 J. Druie (Avon) (9)

5   D. Jevans (Essex) (18)
6   L. Charles (Worcs) (14)
7   G. L. Coles (Middx) (5)
8   C. Drury (Lincs) (20)
9   C. Molesworth (Devon) (12)
10 K. Brasher (Surrey) (16)
11 B. Thompson (Ches) (10)
12 A. Cooper (Kent) (13)
13 J. Placket (Middx) (–)
14 J. Walpole (Surrey) (–)
15 D. Parker (Kent) (–)
16 L. Geeves (Middx) (–)
17 M. Tyler (Kent) (3)
18 I. Locke (Essex) (–)
19 S. Davies (Middx) (–)
20 C. Harrison (Surrey) (19)

British Wimbledon
singles winners

The following British players have won Wimbledon singles titles this century:

Men

1900	Reginald Doherty
1901	Arthur Gore
1902	Laurence Doherty
1903	Laurence Doherty
1904	Laurence Doherty
1905	Laurence Doherty
1906	Laurence Doherty
1908	Arthur Gore
1909	Arthur Gore
1934	Fred Perry
1935	Fred Perry
1936	Fred Perry

Women

1900	Blanche Hillyard
1901	Charlotte Sterry
1902	Muriel Robb
1903	Dorothea Douglass
1904	Dorothea Douglass
1906	Dorothea Douglass
1908	Charlotte Sterry
1909	Dora Boothby
1910	Dorothea Lambert Chambers (née Douglass)
1911	Dorothea Lambert Chambers
1912	Ethel Larcombe
1913	Dorothea Lambert Chambers
1914	Dorothea Lambert Chambers
1924	Kathleen McKane
1926	Kathleen Godfree (née McKane)
1934	Dorothy Round
1937	Dorothy Round
1961	Angela Mortimer
1969	Ann Jones
1977	Virginia Wade

THRILLERS

Best British thrillers

The ten best British thrillers as chosen by Harry Patterson, alias Jack Higgins.

He stresses that because of the great depth of excellence attained by British thriller writers, his 10 favourites are in no particular order.

1 THE HOUND OF THE BASKERVILLES by Sir Arthur Conan Doyle: 'No list would be complete without a Sherlock Holmes story, and this is an excellent example.'

2 THE 39 STEPS by John Buchan: 'Not only a marvellous yarn, but also started a whole trend.'

3 ROGUE MALE by Geoffrey Household: 'Possibly the supreme example of the British thriller at its very best.'

4 THE ODESSA FILE by Frederick Forsyth: 'Happens to be my personal favourite from a marvellous writer, who is far better than his critics give him credit for.'

5 THE IPCRESS FILE by Len Deighton: 'A seminal thriller if ever there was one.'

6 FROM RUSSIA WITH LOVE by Ian Fleming: 'Probably the best example of the work of this great story-teller.'

7 WHEN EIGHT BELLS TOLL by Alastair Maclean: 'The best "straight" thriller from the pen of the master.'

8 THE THIRD MAN by Graham Greene: 'Only a novella, but he does more in this book than anyone else I know can do in 300 pages.'

9 THE SPY WHO CAME IN FROM THE COLD by John Le Carré: 'Still in my opinion head and shoulders above anything else written by Le Carré.'

10 RUNNING BLIND by Desmond Bagley: 'Just about as perfect as the adventure thriller can get.'

TIES

For ten years the Tie Manufacturers' Association has been announcing its Top Tie Men in Britain. The Association, so it says, compiles its list by monitoring newspapers, magazines and television throughout the year. Here are the ten equal winners of 1979 listed in alphabetical order . . .

Top tie men

1 Joel Barnet – MP
2 Frank Bough – BBC commentator
3 Trevor Brooking – West Ham footballer

4 James Callaghan – Leader of the Opposition
5 David Chipp – Editor-in-Chief of the Press Association
6 Sir Derek Ezra – Chairman of the National Coal Board
7 Joe Gormley – President of the National Union of
   Mineworkers
8 Sir Geoffrey Howe – Chancellor of the Exchequer
9 Lawrie McMenemy – Manager of Southampton F.C.
10 Terry Wogan – DJ and TV personality

TOYS

Phillips, the London auctioneers, are often overshadowed by
the bigger boys such as Sotheby's and Christie's when it
comes to breaking records with the sale of Old Masters, but
they have built up a speciality in selling people's more humble
collections. These are some of the world records they broke in
1979, selling objects which until recently were considered
merely toys and trifles.

World records for toys
and other collections

1 *The world's most expensive set of toy soldiers*
A 25-piece group of Salvation Army figures by the
firm of Britain's, including a band and girl with
'The War Cry.' It cost 5/- in the Thirties . . . at auction: £1 450
2 *The world's most expensive single figure by Britain's*
A Thirties version of a village curate from a village
farm set. Originally cost 2d . . .   £80
3 *The world's most expensive teapot*
A rare, 5-inch high red stoneware teapot by the
German maker, Böttger, early 18th-century . . .   £30 000
4 *The world's most expensive used Penny Black stamp,*
1840   £1 150

5 *The world's most expensive run of Wisden's Cricket Almanack*
A run from 1864 to 1969, missing nine volumes, bought by a collector who was short of one single volume . . .   £4 200

6 *The world's most expensive Waterman's fountain pen*
A desk model with which King Edward VIII signed the Instrument of Abdication, £1 in the Thirties . . .   £2 000

7 *The world's most expensive poster*
A Toulouse-Lautrec poster, Divan Japonnais advertising a café concert of 1893, sold at Phillips in New York . . . $19 000

8 *The world's most expensive example of woodworm*
A Flemish oak religious carving of about AD 1500, riddled with woodworm, which had been used for five years by a Home Counties firm of wood preservation specialists to show 'what worm can do to your home'. Rescued from a dustbin . . .   £10 500

Best-selling children's toys, Christmas 1979

List from Hamley's, London, the world's largest toyshop

1 *The Electronic Dashboard* (Hamley's own import)
They stocked up with 15 000 and sold out. Basically, it is a dashboard, including steering wheel with gear stick, which gives out a noise like an engine indicating when to change gear as the revs change. It gets very loud going into fourth.   price: £7 50

2 *Space Lego*
Also completely sold out. The latest in Lego kits, in various sizes and prices.

3 *The Gotz Walking Talking Doll*
. . . which says nursery rhymes. There were several other Walking Talking Dolls which did very well, but this was probably the most popular.   price: £24·50

4 *The Electric Motorbike*
. . . made by an Italian company called Pines.
Runs on a 6-volt battery, suitable for seven-
year-olds and over.   price: £120

5 *Microscopes*
A German one was probably the most popular.
It comes in a wooden box, magnifies 100 to 600
times as well as having a light and a mirror.   price: £19·50

  Motorway toys
. . . were equal fifth in sales, particularly
Scalextric which sells from £24·95 to £200.

6 The Guinness Book of Records
For the first time Hamleys have been
acknowledged in the Guinness book as the
biggest toyshop in the world.   price: £4·25

7 *Hand-held electronic games*
In particular the 'Marksman' which is an owl
with a target and an electronic gun which is
aimed at the target. This is Hamley's own
import. The de luxe model costs . . .   price: £13·65

  The Golf Game
Equal seventh. Looks like a calculator and is
computed to resemble a golf course.   price: £15·95

8 *Water toys*
. . . in particular the 'Playmates' set which
consists of a turtle, alligator and dolphin   price: £1·95

9 Equal ninth: *Horror Masks* which cover your
head   price: £7·95
'Cuby Puzzle,' almost insoluble   price: £5·25
'Bloony', balloons with messages on them   price: £1·65
                                                             for 20

10 *Ping Pong Gun*
Only 48 left out of original stock of 4 000. Large
plastic gun and three table tennis balls   price: £1·25

TRADE UNIONS

Top ten trade unions affiliated to the TUC in order of size of membership, 1979

1	Transport and General Workers' Union	2 072 818
2	Amalgamated Union of Engineering Workers	1 199 465
3	General and Municipal Workers' Union	964 386
4	National and Local Government Officers Association	729 905
5	National Union of Public Employees	712 392
6	Association of Scientific, Technical and Managerial Staffs	471 000
7	Union of Shop, Distributive and Allied Workers	462 178
8	Electrical, Electronic, Telecommunication and Plumbing Union	420 000
9	Union of Construction, Allied Trades and Technicians	320 723
10	National Union of Teachers	291 239

UNEMPLOYMENT IN THE UK

1951	264 000 – 1·3%
1961	347 000 – 1·6%
1971	792 000 – 3·5%
1975	978 000 – 4·1%
1976	1 359 000 – 5·7%
1977	1 484 000 – 6·2%
1978	1 475 000 – 6·2%
1979	1 433 000 – 5·9%

No comments are necessary, except to note a very slight flattening out of the upward curve since 1977.

UNIVERSITIES
(See also Cambridge Colleges and Oxford Colleges)

British universities in order of age

This list consists of universities in England, Scotland and Northern Ireland. The dates refer to their founding as separate universities – though several were founded as colleges before that date. The colleges of the University of Wales are listed separately.

	no. of students
Oxford, 1249	8 781
Cambridge, 1284	9 378
St Andrews, 1411	3 451
Glasgow, 1451	10 515
Aberdeen, 1495	4 816
Edinburgh, 1583	11 250
Durham, 1832	4 211
London, 1836	46 438
Manchester, 1851	15 009
Newcastle, 1852*	7 463
Birmingham, 1880	8 476
Liverpool, 1903	8 138
Leeds, 1904	9 822
Sheffield, 1905	7 432
Queens, Belfast, 1908	5 816
Bristol, 1909	6 006
Reading, 1926	5 990
Nottingham, 1948	5 797
Southampton, 1952	5 988
Hull, 1954	5 134
Exeter, 1955	5 045
Leicester, 1957	4 226
Sussex, 1961	4 575

*Originally part of Durham University.

Keele, 1962	2 805
East Anglia (Norwich), 1963	4 061
York, 1963	2 650
Strathclyde, 1964	6 402
Lancaster, 1964	4 196
Essex, 1964	2 786
Ulster, 1965	1 570
Warwick, 1965	5 099
Kent (Canterbury), 1965	3 747
Heriot-Watt, 1966	3 132
Loughborough, 1966	5 760
Aston (Birmingham), 1966	5 711
The City University, 1966	3 224
Brunel, 1966	4 450
Bath, 1966	3 017
Bradford, 1966	4 250
Surrey, 1966	2 839
Dundee, 1967	2 911
Stirling, 1967	2 471
Salford, 1967	4 014

University of Wales, 1893

	no. of students
Aberystwyth	2 633
Bangor	2 452
Cardiff, Institute of Science and Technology	2 457
Cardiff, National School of Medicine	661
Cardiff, University College	4 284
Lampeter	643
Swansea	3 116

University courses, UK, 1975-6

		percentage
Courses taken by full-time undergraduates:		
1	Social, administrative and business studies	23·5
2	Science	23·0
3	Engineering and technology	13·8
4	Language, literature and area studies	12·8
5	Medicine, dentistry and health	11·9
6	Arts other than languages	10·3
7	Agriculture, forestry and veterinary science	1·9
8	Architecture and other professional and vocational subjects	1·8
9	Education	1·0

UNMARRIEDS

Famous British people who never married

Elizabeth I – queen
Jane Austen – novelist
Charles Lamb – essayist
Sir Isaac Newton – mathematician
Florence Nightingale – hospital reformer
Alexander Pope – poet
Adam Smith – economist
Edward Heath – prime minister (up to now)
L. S. Lowry – artist
Lewis Carroll – writer

VALENTINES

The posh newspapers have created a new line in classified advertising in recent years – charging their readers a large sum to wish each other soppy or sexy sentiments every 14 February, St Valentine's Day. Both *The Times* and *The Guardian* devoted several pages to Valentines in 1980. Most of the messages were to do with animals – Cuddly Bear wanting to curl up with Fluffytail, or Bunny hoping to be liked by Pussy.

A reader of *The Guardian*, Alison Turnbull of Wimbledon, an area well-known for its animal life, analysed all the valentines to find out which animal was the most popular with *Guardian* readers in their fantasy life.

Guardian readers' favourite Valentine animal

	animal	mentions	including
1	Bear	55	Teddy, Pooh, Rupert but no Paddington or Fozzie
2	Pig	41	Miss Piggy, Porkchop, Piglet, Hambone, Willy Grunt
3	Cat	33	Pussy, Moggie, Kat, Felix
4	Dog	19	Woofs, Puppy, Beagle but only one Snoopy
5	Rabbit	13	Rabbit, Bunny, Lapin, Fluffytail
6	Tiger	10	Tigger
7	Frog	9	2 Kermits only
8	Mole	8	—
9	Rat	7	3 Ratbags, Ratty
10	Bee	5	—

There were also two Iguanas, three Aardvarks, four Kippers, two Penguins, three Ferrets and two Coypu. Ms Turnbull drew the conclusions that A. A. Milne was forever popular, but Miss Piggy had clearly fallen out with Kermit since last year. She thought that Kenneth Grahame and John Le Carré could fight out number 8 between themselves.

VENEREAL DISEASE

Department of Health, reproduced with the permission of the Controller of HMSO

Sexually-transmitted diseases: patients seen at hospital clinics* in England and Wales, 1976

		no. of cases
All cases dealt with for the	male	247 445
first time at any centre	female	159 703
syphilis	male	3 380
	female	1 075
gonorrhoea	male	37 793
	female	22 289
other conditions requiring treatment	male	145 020
	female	99 576
other conditions not requiring treatment	male	61 252
	female	36 763

*New cases seen during the year

VILLAINS

Lesser known British villains
(in no particular order)
Jonathon Green, compiler of The Directory of Infamy

1 **Kate Webster** Preferred drinking to housework. She killed her employer after being told off, then dismembered the corpse, boiled up the flesh and dumped it by the river near Hammersmith. She sold the rendered human dripping around the local pubs. Arrested in her native Ireland in 1879, she was hanged.

2 **Sawney Beane** The Beane family – some forty-six, all incestuous, flourished near Galloway, Scotland, in the late

fourteenth century. At the time of their capture in 1435 they had killed and robbed some 1 000 victims. The authorities caught up with them and the family were killed slowly and painfully. Their victims' corpses, butchered and smoked, festooned the Beane's cavernous HQ.

3 The Reverend Harold Davidson, Rector of Stiffkey. The hapless cleric was discovered consorting with London prostitutes, thus scandalizing his Norfolk parish in the 1930s. He was defrocked and turned to show-business, appearing in a tub and placing his head in a lion's mouth in fairgrounds round the country. The lion duly shut its jaws one sad day in Skegness.

4 Mary Ann Cotton Britain's premiere mass murderer managed at least sixteen and probably twenty-one victims – all close relatives – between 1852 and 1872. All apparently suffered from 'gastric fever'. Mary was hanged in 1873, a job which was bungled and took three minutes.

5 Richard Rosse Rosse was cook to the Bishop of Rochester in 1531. For undisclosed reasons he poisoned some seventeen of the bishop's guests at a dinner. Rosse was boiled to death for his crime.

6 Horace Rayner Rayner was the unacknowledged illegitimate son of William Whiteley, 'the Universal Provider' and founder of Whiteley's department store in Queensway, W2. In 1907 he walked into his father's office, argued with him, then shot him dead. Whiteley's motto 'Add conscience to your capital' had not extended to his private life, but 20 000 people signed a petition and saved him from the gallows. Rayner still served twelve years.

7 Arthur Furguson Furguson, an erstwhile actor, used his talents for special solo performances. He sold Nelson's column at £6 000 a time, and 'rented out' Buckingham Palace and the Tower of London. In 1925 he moved to America. After many successes he was jailed when he failed to sell the Statue of Liberty for $100 000. Released from jail in 1930, he vanished.

8 **Mary Tofts** In 1726 this simple country girl from Godalming, Surrey, managed to persuade a large number of people who should have known better that she had given birth to rabbits. She produced a number of litters and convinced even M St André, the king's surgeon. Finally the imposture was discovered and she was packed off to the country.

WATER

In the average British household (of four people) each person uses over 12 000 gallons of water a year. This is where it goes.

Water (gallons per year per person)

Lavatory	4 560
Washing and bathing	4 560
Drinking and cooking	365
Dishwasher and cleaning	1 280
Laundry	1 280
Garden	550
Car washing	182
	12 777

WEALTH

To be one of the richest 1% of the UK population in 1977 you needed net wealth of at least £60 000. To be part of the richest 10% you needed only £13 500.

Over the period 1966–74, the share of national wealth held by the top 10% dropped by 11% (from 68·7 to 57·5). Since 1974, it has slightly crept back again and the top 10% now own 61·1%, possibly due to the huge increase in house values.

All the same, 50% of the population still owns 95% of the wealth.

Distribution of wealth
in the UK

Inland Revenue

percentages of wealth

			1966	1971	1974	1975	1976	1977
Most wealthy	1%	of population	33·0	30·5	22·5	23·5	23·7	24·0
"	2%	" "	41·7	38·7	29·6	30·5	31·5	32·2
"	5%	" "	55·7	51·8	43·1	43·8	46·1	46·4
"	10%	" "	68·7	65·1	57·5	58·0	61·4	61·1
"	25%	" "	86·9	86·5	83·6	83·3	84·2	83·9
"	50%	" "	96·5	97·2	92·9	93·3	95·4	95·0
Least	50%	" "	3·5	2·8	7·1	6·7	4·6	5·0
Total wealth of the population (thousand million)			107	164	236	272	296	345

WEST END SHOWS

In January 1979, *No Sex Please We're British* became the longest-running comedy in the history of the London theatre, beating all previous comedies. It celebrated its ninth year in June 1980.

Longest-running comedies

1 *No Sex Please We're British* – 3 757 performances (up to 1 June 1980)
2 *Life With Father* – 3 213 performances
3 *There's A Girl In My Soup* – 2 517 performances
4 *Boeing-Boeing* – 2 035 performances
5 *Blithe Spirit* – 1 997 performances
6 *Worm's Eye View* – 1 745 performances
7 *Reluctant Heroes* – 1 610 performances

Longest-running
current shows

West End shows, still running in 1980, with their total number of performances.

1 *The Mousetrap* – 28th year
   11 307 performances (as of 2 February 1980)
   The world's longest running show ever.
2 *Jesus Christ Superstar* – 9 years in June 1980
   3 126 performances (as of 4 February 1980)
3 *No Sex Please We're British* – 9 years in June 1980
   3 611 performances (as of 5 February 1980)
4 *Oliver* – 3 runs
   Total number of performances 3 836 (as of 5 February 1980)
   1st run – New Theatre, June 1960–66
   2 618 performances
   2nd run – Piccadilly Theatre, April 1967–8
   311 performances
   3rd run – Albery Theatre, December 1977 onwards
   894 performances (as of 5 February 1980)

Other London productions
which have run for more
than 1 000 performances

The Black and White Minstrel Show	4 344
Oliver (1st run)	2 618
The Sound of Music	2 386
Salad Days	2 283
My Fair Lady	2 281
Chu-Chin-Chow	2 238
Charlie Girl	2 202
The Boy Friend	2 084
Boeing-Boeing	2 035
Fiddler On the Roof	2 030

WHISKY

Each year, 16 million cases of Scotch whisky are drunk in Britain. Here are the ten biggest-selling brands:

The ten biggest-selling
whisky brands

1 Bells
2 Teachers
3 Haig
4 Famous Grouse
5 Standfast
6 Claymore
7 White Horse
8 Langs
9 Long John
19 Whyte Mackay

Tax on whisky

	(estimated tax as % of retail price)
UK	78%
Canada	66%
France	62%
Belgium	57%
Italy	51%
Australia ⎱ Spain ⎰	50%
W. Germany	44%
Japan	41%
USA	38%

A disgusting list, and one which we should be ashamed to top. Whose whisky is it anyway?

WORDS

New words of the Seventies

Twenty new words which have come into prominence in the 1970s, as selected by Dr R. W. Burchfield, chief editor of the Oxford English dictionaries. Most of these words have recently appeared in the various new editions of the Oxford dictionaries, except for three which have yet to appear in any English dictionary.

1 *Ayatollah*, a Muslim religious leader in Iran.

2 *Go bananas*, (slang) to go crazy.

3 *Bionic*, (of a person or his faculties) operated by electronic means, not naturally.

4 *Biorhythm*, any of the recurring cycles of physical, emotional and intellectual activity said to occur in people's lives.

5 *Eurodollar*, dollar held in bank in Europe etc., not in USA.

6 *Granny flat*, a flat in someone's house where an elderly relative can live independently but close to the family.

7 *Green pound*, the agreed value of the £ according to which payments to agricultural producers are reckoned in the EEC.

8 *Hatchback*, a car with a sloping back hinged at the top so that it can be opened; the back itself.

9 *Kneecapping*, shooting in the legs to lame a person as a punishment.

10 *Lassa fever*, acute febrile virus disease of tropical Africa.

11 *Minimum lending rate*, the announced minimum rate (influencing other rates of interest) at which the Bank of England lends or advances money.

12 *No-go area*, an area to which entry is forbidden to certain people or groups.

13 *Plea bargaining*, practice of agreeing to drop charge(s), or to sentence leniently, if the accused pleads guilty to other charge(s).

14 *Poverty trap*, the condition of being so dependent on State benefits that an increase in one's income merely means that one loses some of these and is no better off.

15 *Punk rock*, a type of pop music involving outrage and shock effects in music, behaviour and dress.
16 *Quadraphonic*, (of sound reproduction) using four transmission channels.
17 *Quango*, from the initials of quasi-autonomous non-governmental organization.
18 *Secondary picketing*, picketing of a place other than one's own place of work during a trade union dispute.
19 *Shuttle diplomacy*, negotiations conducted by a mediator who travels to several countries at brief intervals.
20 *Skateboard*, a small board with wheels like those of roller-skates, for riding on (as a sport) while standing.

The three new words still to appear in any Oxford dictionary are ayatollah (a 1979 arrival), biorhythm and secondary picketing.

Alan Coren's
favourite words, 1980

Mr Coren, the editor of *Punch*, goes off words, as most people go off things they use every day, but at the same time he suddenly becomes very fond of certain words, often for no particular reason. In the year of Our Lord 1980, these were ten of the words he was most fond of.

ozalid	peristaltic
hone	weevil
widdle	moby
Eustachian	nympholept
ferret	prat

'Ozalid' is a sort of photocopy and it's simply the sound he likes. 'Hone,' 'ferret', 'weevil' and 'moby' he likes purely for the feel of the words. He likes 'widdle,' meaning pee, for the noise it makes. As for the long words he has chosen, 'Eustachian' refers to the tubes which connect the nose to the ear and he likes it because it sounds like Euston station; 'peristaltic' refers to the movement of the intestines, and 'nympholept' is someone who, like him, constantly desires the unobtainable. As for 'prat', that old-fashioned but rather mild schoolboyish term of abuse, well, he thinks it is just a rather wonderful word.

X-CERTIFICATE FILMS

These are the ten top rated X-films, in terms of popularity and box office success, at the Dilly Cinema, Piccadilly, London W1, during 1979:

1 *Baby Rosemary*
2 *Inside Jennifer Welles*
3 *Sex World*
4 *First Time*
5 *Blue Climax*
6 *Tapestry of Passion*
7 *Portrait of Seduction*
8 *Cream Dreams*
9 *Hot and Randy*
10 *Bizarre Desires*

A spokesman for the Dilly wouldn't give figures regarding money or audience ratings but said: 'The more explicit the films the more popular they are.' The majority of complaints he gets are that films are not explicit enough. Britain has a stricter censorship than Sweden or America, or even France, which is supposedly a Catholic country. X-rated films in the UK are watched by more men than women, although quite a few women are now going to see blue movies, sometimes on their own, or with a friend. The popular stereotype of the dirty old raincoat brigade is a myth, so the spokesman stoutly maintained. 'The Dilly gets a lot of businessmen, young people and tourists coming to see its films.' So there . . .

218

Extra X-films

Some of the other X-films currently on show in London in 1980, chosen for their interesting titles rather than any artistic content.

1 *She's Seventeen And Anxious*
2 *Everybody Loves Big Ones*
3 *I'm Not Feeling Myself Tonight*
4 *Ups and Downs of a Girl on Holiday*
5 *Banging in Bangkok*
6 *French Undressing*
7 *Emmanuelle Meets the Wife-Swappers*
8 *Come Play With Me*
9 *School of Hard Knocks*
10 *What the ˄ Swedish Butler Saw*

YOUTH

Top youth clubs and organizations

The Girl Guide and Boy Scout Associations continue to have the largest memberships, but the membership of youth clubs has also grown steadily.

		thousands
1	Girl Guides	360
	Boy Scouts	235
2	National Association of Youth Clubs:	
	boys	341
	girls	251
3	Boys' Brigade	147
	Girls' Brigade	103

4 YMCA	34
YWCA	17
5 Army Cadet Corps	44
6 Combined Cadet Force	44
7 Air Training Corps	35
8 Crusaders: boys } girls	22
9 Sea Cadet Corps	19
10 Community Service Volunteers	8·1
11 Outward Bound Trust: men	6·1
women	1·2

ZOOS

The most popular
animals at London Zoo

In 1979, 1 600 000 people visited London Zoo – 33% were children, 40% were from overseas – and these are the animals which most people went to see.

	% of visitors
Monkeys and apes	80
Giant pandas	75
Lions	60
Tigers	60
Giraffes	45
Bears	40
Insects	30
Reptiles	30

The days of individual animals who became superstars in their own right seem to be over for the moment. In the 1950s Brumas the polar bear, London Zoo's all time great, brought in one million visitors a year. Next came Chi Chi, the giant panda in the Sixties, and then the late and greatly mourned Guy the gorilla in the Seventies.

There are two named giant pandas at present, Ching Ching and Chia Chia, but neither has caught on with the public. Zoo officials hope desperately that a baby panda will appear in the Eighties and bring in the crowds.

Total annual figures at London Zoo dropped in the Seventies, from two million in 1971 to 1·6 million in 1979. There are now 150 zoos, safari parks and bird gardens open to the public in the UK, attracting 15 million visitors a year.

LAST LIST

A list of the lists
Jasper Carrott would like
to have seen in this book

1 Helmets of the Second World War in chronological order.
2 The ten most popular garden gnomes.
3 The ten favourite road signs.
4 The ten best-read telephone directories.
5 The ten favourite neuroses.
6 The most popular football chants.
7 The smallest classifiable particles of food.
   ('You know, rice, popcorn, pepper grains, semolina . . .')
8 The most used profanities.
9 The ten most popular estate agents.
10 The ten lowest wage-earners in Britain.
11 The ten most difficult to find ex-directory phone numbers.
12 The most-often dialled phone number.
13 The ten most boring jobs.

Well, we did try with some of them. They must all be findable. The nearest we got was with the number 12, the most-often dialled phone number, one answer to which is under 'T' for Telephone. Perhaps next time we'll manage the rest. Meantime, if you have any British lists of any sort, which you think might amuse or interest a wider public, please send them.

Yours, listlessly,
Hunter Davies.